INCEST

Perfection is not the land you leave,
It is the pole you measure from; it gives
Geography to your ways and wanderings.

Norman Nicholson, 'To a Child Before Birth', from *Rock Face*

INCEST
A NEW PERSPECTIVE

MARY HAMER

polity

First published in 2002 by Polity Press in association with Blackwell Publishers Ltd,
a Blackwell Publishing Company.

Editorial office:
Polity Press
65 Bridge Street
Cambridge CB2 1UR, UK

Marketing and production:
Blackwell Publishers Ltd
108 Cowley Road
Oxford OX4 1JF, UK

Published in the USA by
Blackwell Publishers Inc.
350 Main Street
Malden, MA 02148, USA

A catalogue record for this book is available from the British Library.

Library of Congress Cataloging-in-Publication Data
Hamer, Mary, 1944–
    Incest : a new perspective / Mary Hamer.
        p. cm.
    Includes index.
    ISBN 0-7456-2415-4 — ISBN 0-7456-2416-2 (pbk.)
    1. Incest.   2. Incest in literature.   3. Incest in popular culture.
4. Child sexual abuse.   I. Title.
HV6570.6 .H35 2002
306.877—dc21
                                                    2001006166
Typeset in 11 on 13 pt Berling
by Graphicraft Ltd., Hong Kong
Printed in Great Britain by TJ International, Padstow, Cornwall

This book is printed on acid-free paper.

For Nick

Contents

PART II
On Being Reminded

Preface

I am grateful to all my friends for the patience with which they listened as I found my way through the process of writing this book but my thanks go in particular to Mary Bernard. I owe a special debt to Carol Gilligan, for sharing her own work on love with me and for her refusal to let me forget the question of pleasure. David Held has played the part of an ideal publisher: liberating me by asking what book I would write about incest if I were free to write exactly as I wanted and then forbearing to hurry me as I worked.

It was at Harvard, in the Department of Afro-American Studies, that the ideas for this book germinated and that most of it was written. There the work of Werner Sollors drew to my attention the overlap between responses to incest and responses to inter-racial sex. In that Cambridge too Judith Herman was kind enough to meet with me and to respond patiently to my questions: without her work and the work of other pioneering therapists this book could not have been written.

Only those who know me can appreciate how much I owe to the generosity of my husband. Yet writing about incest is an act to bring one's own family under a cloud, as he would remind me wistfully, asking whether I 'couldn't work on something more wholesome'. I don't expect that my argument will please everyone but I do mean to make it accessible to all. For this reason I have avoided footnotes and kept notes and bibliographical information to a minimum. They can be found at the back of the book.

Acknowledgements

The extract from Norman Nicholson's poem 'To a Child before Birth' (*Rock Face*, London 1948) is reproduced by kind permission of David Higham Associates.

The illustrations on pages 138 and 145 are reproduced by kind permission of Photofest. Copyright © Columbia Pictures Corporation. The illustrations on pages 112, 113, 115, 117, 122, 127, 129, 131, 132, 134, 140, 141, 143 and 147 are from the collection of The Museum of Modern Art, New York.

Introduction

Late in the day

Looking back on myself as a schoolgirl, I feel confused. At the time, it was my impression that I liked being at school. Yet when I revisited those days through the act of writing, I found that a different story began to emerge. When I began writing a memoir of my childhood, around the time when I turned fifty, I was not yet aware of what was prompting me. But on going back in the summer of 2000 to a reunion at St Paul's Roman Catholic Grammar School for Girls, after decades away from it, I listened to the voices of the women who had been my classmates between the ages of eleven and eighteen. It seemed that we had each come armed with the same question. We turned to each other, asking 'What was wrong with this place?' The wonder is that it took so many years for us to ask.

These days, the long time-lag between trauma and the perception of its effects is generally recognized. Television and newspapers have helped to spread information: the idea of the flashback has become familiar. Like others, I had absorbed the notion that past experience can intrude into the life of the present by means of fragmented images or waves of feeling which arrive unbidden in the mind, as part of the mind's attempt to reconstruct itself after shock. Like them I thought of trauma sufferers as different from myself. It was the victims of incest or of sexual abuse, the veterans of war or political terrorism, and those who had been witness to horrific events who were named by Judith Herman in her book *Trauma and Recovery*. But when I found myself experiencing such a flashback, in connection with the first steps in my own religious education as a child, that gave me pause for thought. It suggested a link that I had not suspected between religious teaching and abuse.

I knew that I had no personal experience of incest or sexual abuse, or of the other experiences usually associated with trauma. Yet this flashback, which I will describe in due course, occurred after I had already spent months in reading about trauma and in trying to see a pattern. Was there any connection, I found myself asking, between the experiences that give rise to trauma and are taken as exceptional and those which are accepted as wholesome and commonplace? Arriving as if in response to that question, my own flashback prompted me to think again about what I knew concerning the education which I had received as a girl. I began to ask myself whether I should I be reading that education itself as a form of abuse.

Having come to find something gratuitous in all the mystery that shrouds incest, I was prepared to believe that a piece of the puzzle might have been lost, a crucial aspect of the question hidden from view. Taking up this cue, I began to ask myself about my own mind and about the way in which it had been formed. I began to wonder about knowing and to ask what it was that I knew in the days before I set foot in school. I discovered a break between the picture of the world that I had built up for myself as a young child and the picture that my teachers offered.

As one in a whole classroom of girls, I knew that I was not alone. Other classrooms, other girls educated in the same western tradition might be no different. As grown women, their minds too might still be harbouring the effects of an old shock. With this notion, I discovered a connection between my own experience and that of other women, including the women of whom I was writing in the context of incest. This gave me the form for my argument: viewing the education of girls in terms of abuse, I take that as the starting point for thinking about incest.

The writer Anton Chekhov once explained that the work of the artist is to state a problem correctly: 'In Anna Karenin and Evgeny Onegin not a single problem is solved but they satisfy you completely because all the problems are correctly stated in them.' Like these tragic stories from Russia, tales of incest or abuse also concern love and the place where love breaks down. It might seem that the problem of incest had already been adequately stated, in that many people now accept both that incest occurs and that it is usually associated with damage. But there remain voices of dissent, voices that speak of false memory or claim that incest is a refined form of pleasure, voices too which ask whether incest is always wrong. These attitudes resist integration with each other, suggesting that a satisfactory statement of the problem has yet to be made. This is not just a problem of aesthetics. There is no evidence to suggest that the threat of punishment is effective in preventing abuse. Without understanding exactly what is causing the breakdown of love to which acts of abuse draw our attention we are in no position to prevent such acts from recurring.

Starting out with my own story of an inner life that school silenced and comparing that with the stories of relationship told by two other educated women, the film-maker Jennifer Montgomery and the writer Sappho Durrell, I present the discussion of incest in a new frame. With this frame in place, a new look can also be taken at the education of boys and at the experience of adult men. For that I draw on the evidence presented by the work of film-maker Louis Malle in his movie which features incest, *Murmur of the Heart*, and on the widely reported case of Father James Porter, the Catholic priest who in 1992 was charged with sexual abuse in Massachusetts.

Unfamiliar as this line of approach may appear, a body of theory to support it has been in existence since before the Second World War in the writings of two pioneering analysts, Ian Suttie and Sandòr Ferenczi. Even before the 1950s when John Bowlby's study of refugee children demonstrated that children need close and tender contact to keep them alive and eager for life, Ian Suttie and Sandòr Ferenczi were drawing attention to the experience of education, in order to ask about its harmful effects. I quote Suttie's work on early childhood in a follow-up to the story of my own experience as a young child, as a gloss on that account and in order to support my claim that such experience is not unique. In Ferenczi's work on incest, religious education is considered in the context of abuse. His writings are brought forward following my discussion of the Father Porter case, where they offer support for a reading that does not seek to settle blame on a single offender but points beyond that to institutions and features which are systemic. Ferenczi's account of abuse with its inner dynamic offers a map, one which serves to order and bring into relationship the stories that have been discussed so far. Writing of the lofty detachment of the authoritarian attitude, he demonstrates unsuspected links between sexual abuse and certain forms of moral or religious teaching, and also with conventional psychoanalysis.

To bring the first half of my argument to a close, I turn to the work of two contemporary analysts based in London, Valerie Sinason and Estela Welldon. Each writes about working with clients who have a history of sexual abuse, describing how this work has required her to break out of the professional mindset and the techniques in which she had been trained, or as I would put it myself, to stop reproducing the old system and the old attitudes passed on by means of formal education. Sinason lays her emphasis on the need for a change of attitude on the therapist's part, in order to avoid censoring both their patients and themselves. On the basis of thirty years' experience in working with these clients, Welldon has gone still further to make a structural change. She no longer treats them in a one-to-one setting, where old patterns of confusion around intimate relationship are too readily played out, but meets with them in groups. In this new setting those who have a history as victims are mixed in with others who have a history of committing abuse, an arrangement which subtly refuses to make the old judgements that draw a line between the sheep and the goats. Dropping the role of judge and dethroning herself as the voice of wisdom Welldon takes it as her function in these groups to support clear thinking and to promote the safety of all members. In this structure it is the voice of the group and the group dynamic that determine the course of events.

These conditions are the ones that she has found most favourable to the recovery of those who have been involved in abuse. In making these innovations, as Welldon explains, she was responding to the evidence of her own experience. I myself, however, cannot avoid noticing that her move could also be described in terms of structures that are political: she takes a step towards a form of organization that has a lot in common with democracy, or at least with what we understand as the democratic ideal, where the voice of every speaker counts. Here we come up against a paradox, for it appears that the working conditions which she describes are very different from those which pertain in the world outside, in spite of the fact that this world is said to be governed by democracy. It is conditions outside that have given rise to the acts of abuse which led clients to seek help.

The second part of the book takes up this paradox, suggesting that there are some who are not deceived by the official account of the forms that govern our lives. Putting my faith in art and in the scepticism of the artist, I turn to fictionalized accounts. In movies I find a picture of the world which is put together using the first language of the psyche, the language of images. Watching movies, we share a form of knowledge that no one needs special training to pick up. It was as a viewer myself, a spectator in the cinema audience, that I first registered that there might be a pattern which had not been identified behind acts of incest, one that lay behind the stories of individual experience, connecting them with the structures of everyday life. I have chosen for exploration five works of art that feature incest and abuse. Three are movies and two are novels: *Suddenly Last Summer*, *Through a Glass Darkly*, *Lolita*, *The Bluest Eye* and *The God of Small Things*.

If you ask why an artist should depict something as painful as incest, I reply that this question seems to be turning the matter upside down. In setting out to state the problem of incest correctly such artists are offering pleasure to their viewers, the pleasure of forming an understanding which is more accurate and more complete, or to put it more simply, helping them to know. But as a process, coming to know can be a painful one. Undoing ignorance, as artists have so often found, may involve provoking anger and dismay, even temporary confusion, as old models of thinking come apart. When I set out in search of this great pleasure, wanting to know, I did not imagine the resistance in myself that I would uncover. It is with the day when a newspaper report brought me face to face with my own resistance to clear thinking on the subject of incest, a resistance that I found to be widely shared, that I begin.

Part I

On Knowing and Not Wanting To Know

Intimacy and Pleasure

On my way home to Cambridge in the summer of 1992, after a year spent away in the United States, seated in the train, scanning through a London evening paper to find out what I had missed, I came on a reference to the suicide of Sappho Durrell. The article implied that her incestuous relationship with her father, the writer Lawrence Durrell, lay behind it. Lawrence Durrell was famous as a novelist and poet: Sappho herself had published a few reviews but at thirty-five, the age she had reached when she killed herself, her own career as a writer was still embryonic. For me, as for many readers of *The Alexandria Quartet*, the work which had made her father famous, its tale of an incestuous romance between the poet Pursewarden and his blind sister Liza had been just that, a romantic fiction, something that existed in a magic realm outside time. Now with this grainy photograph, the heavy inking of the page, for me the romance of the notion shattered like glass.

Durrell's account of two children growing up together in a remote farmhouse in Ireland, alone except for an old woman who took care of them, once read innocently to me, almost like a fairy-tale. Around 1960 when the Alexandria novels were being published, for most people incest could still be contained within the category of fiction. Specialists really knew better, of course, but faced with the challenge of what they knew they drew back. When a young psychologist named John Bowlby did make a move to work on incest, not long after the Second World

War, he was warned off it by senior members of his profession and told that it would sabotage his career to make a study of a subject that there was such resistance to knowing about. Instead, he chose to work on maternal deprivation and so made his name.

We have had to give up our pretence of ignorance in recent years and agree to face the fact that sexual relations between close relatives do take place, and not only in the west. Tracking the path of HIV infection in India, for example, threw up unsuspected patterns of sexual connection within families even before a recent survey suggested that among educated women up to 76 per cent had been subjected to sexual abuse at home. Nor is it safe to think of this as a new problem: after interviewing people who as children had been evacuated away from the bombing during the Second World War, Charles Wheeler, the BBC correspondent, estimated that 1 in 10 had been abused in their new homes. Figures are only starting to become available around the globe but there seems no reason to believe that there is any country in which incest does not occur with some regularity, even though in theory it is forbidden. In many countries national pride intensifies the pressure for secrecy which is already exerted within families, because it has been the conventional wisdom to equate acts of incest with the absence of civilized values. It is often claimed that civilization is based on the taboo on incest, that this taboo stands at the centre of the human world.

Language itself, like shame, seems to block clear thinking in this area. Most of us understand the term 'incest' as referring to sexual relations that are forbidden because there is a blood tie between the partners already. But in spite of the fact that they are covered by a blanket term, it seems obvious that the relationships which are covered by the single term 'incest' take many different forms, involving situations and events which have little in common. What adolescents experience when they become incestuously involved raises issues that are very different from those raised by the brutal penetration of a young child. And what about when it takes place between two free adults? As a topic, incest confronts us with questions about pleasure even while it asks that we also bear in mind trauma and damage. This demand seems to paralyse our minds.

It is perhaps not surprising if many of us baulk at imagining the state of mind or the circumstances in which an older person could force themselves sexually on a child. But this need not any longer be allowed to distract us from a more pressing task, that is, the work of examining the state of mind, or rather the state of dissociation, that exists inside our own heads. We might ask ourselves how it comes about that what has been considered as universally forbidden, a taboo that exists in every culture, seems by all accounts to be a world-wide practice. By what means has our common blindness been preserved?

Finding answers to this question will take up the first part of this book. Whether every act of incest is automatically an act of abuse is a matter that has also been blurred. Both women and men have spoken repeatedly of the trauma, the humiliation and confusion that they experienced as very young people when they were used to secure sexual gratification for an adult, a parent or parental figure, someone older or more powerful than them-selves. It is true that the majority of reported cases do involve fathers and daughters, where the disparity in terms of power and authority is likely to be very great, but it is also clear that not all incestuous encounters are between those who are not equals.

Siblings of about the same age, whether same-sex or hetero-sexual like Durrell's pair, the twins Liza and Pursewarden, might be pretty equally matched. In cases where there is no disparity, no overwhelming of one person's authority by another's, there appears to be no reason why trauma should arise, were it not for the pressure of the ban which defines all forms of incest as wrong. This pressure once internalized by individuals could be enough to give rise to the traumatic fears which are linked with the terror of retribution. As a form of damage, psychological trauma is associated with helplessness, with being unable to resist or escape from situations of extreme danger so that the psycho-logical integrity of the individual is put at risk. In cases of incestu-ous abuse it is the forcing, not the close family relationship, which does the damage. Incest and abuse are not synonymous. This would suggest that there is no reason to intervene in those situations where a brother and sister decide to live together as partners. Their greatest danger at present seems to be the isola-tion entailed by the secrecy they are obliged to adopt. Yet in Michigan a few years ago a sibling couple were jailed. Attitudes to incest that focus on punishment and on enforcing isolation are often found, especially in those in authority: I shall be arguing however, that thinking in terms of punishment is to step even more deeply into confusion.

It is not even clear that all cases of abuse are equally traumatic, although the pressure in favour of blanket condemnation is intense. 'Dare one suggest, in the present climate of opinion, that the context of sexual interchange between adult and child – the presence of love or hate, the degree of confusion, etc. – is of major importance?', as the psychoanalyst and author Peter Lomas enquired in the *Times Literary Supplement* on 2 December 1994. It appears that there are families in which the shared closeness of a sexualized relationship that might otherwise be defined as abusive offers the only refuge, the only experience of tenderness. In those conditions, even an abusive relationship can be a life-saver. In the 1997 play *How I Learned to Drive*, American playwright Paula Vogel presents such a family, where the uncle was sexually involved with his niece from the time she was nine.

Without denying that damage was done to her, the play suggests that if it were not for this relationship this girl might not have survived her family, to leave home and go away to college. This escape also means that she develops and chooses to withdraw from the sexual relationship with her uncle. The play is titled *How I Learned to Drive*: it is this uncle who gives her the literal driving lessons which allow her to leave town. The uncle and his story also have their own weight for this playwright. He is a sensitive man, isolated in a marriage and a family where emotion is coarsened or blanked out in the other adults, and so finding rewarding exchanges only with the children. Without the hope that the relationship with his niece gave him, once she has refused the marriage that he was planning to offer her at eighteen, this uncle then drinks himself to death.

As a piece of theatre *How I Learned to Drive* presented these stories side by side on the stage, showing how one was bound up in the other and that neither was intelligible without information about the family as a whole. Instead of drawing back in affront, when they were invited to be present in the company of live actors who were performing this situation and bringing it to life for them, audiences responded with recognition. *How I Learned to Drive* was awarded a Pulitzer Prize. Writing in antiquity, another dramatist, the African playwright Terence, had already remarked: 'Homo sum: humani nil a me alienum puto' – which could be paraphrased as 'I will draw back from nothing that teaches me about human nature.' Watching *How I Learned to Drive*, theatregoers were not moved to disgust but to recognition and to reflection.

Unlike the language of theatre, the language of educated think-ing shies away from exploring the human meaning of the experi-ence. Theatre plays on voice and on the difference between voices. As a visual art it also plays on what can be observed by the audience and on the gap between word and action, between what is hap-pening on stage and the way that action is spoken of by the characters. Stimulated by this to check the evidence for consist-ency, audience members are actively invited to know. In com-parison with that, arguments about incest which are primarily intellectual, and are not grounded in an appeal to the evidence of the senses, tend to run into the sand.

Even among therapists, work with 'incest survivors' – a term which obscures the fate of those, like Sappho Durrell, who do not survive abuse – is allowed to cover over the complexity of what is at stake when incest occurs. In 1998 two biographers pub-lished lives of Lawrence Durrell and both chose to side-step the matter of his relationship with his daughter Sappho, one with talk of 'false memory syndrome' and the other speaking of the need for 'proof'. These terms might be read as the language of scientific thinking, but when they are used as they are here, in biography, where telling the story of a life is the task at hand, they seem designed to mask an inability to think or to know once the topic of incest has been raised.

Literary critics appear tacitly to accept Durrell's own writings about incest as an extension of his enquiry into pleasure, but a nod in passing is all that these critics seem to manage, not as if they were hostile but as though they were shy. It is as though they were not certain how to go on, how to find language or even whether they hoped to be understood. 'Carrying within it the notion of intellectual as well as sexual incest and homosexuality which are predicates of this initial flashback, *The Avignon Quintet* thus returns us to the organic connection between sexual and intellectual intercourse, of which the *pogon*, the "word which does not exist", might be regarded as both "the compact and the seed"', writes Richard Pine, in his book *Lawrence Durrell: The Mindscape*. Such ambivalence may be no accident, for under Christianity pleasure has been linked with the forbidden. It is not always remembered – or perhaps we have forbidden ourselves to remember – that we were introduced to our capacity for pleasure as infants in the care of adults.

The intimacy between parents and babies or young children, an intimacy that is usually associated with mothers, is the earliest form of pleasure that we know. Such pleasure is no luxury, as John Bowlby himself showed in the study of refugee children that he made soon after the war, but our natural medium or habitat, our way of connecting with the world and with ourselves. Without this closeness children fail to develop and become listless and sick. They lose interest in the world and their curiosity, which is another name for their intelligence, dies back. By his work, Bowlby showed that in the human blueprint pleasure and knowing, knowing and intimacy are linked. It is in the cradle of this intimacy as young children that we learn to know and become eager to explore the world.

The company of women

Like the critics who write about Lawrence Durrell, I received a training in the study of literature in the course of my education at the university. Noting how the impulse to explore seems to wither away in older, more educated minds at the mention of the word incest, and remembering the healthy curiosity of children, I propose to adopt a new tack and call on what I knew as a child. Looking back at myself at the time when I was small, before I was trained as a reader, I find myself thinking about fairy-tales and about the Emperor's new clothes. I wonder about the world that is seen through a child's eyes and I ask: what could I see for myself as a young child?

Streetsbrook Road stretches out in front of me. I can see all the way down to the roundabout as I speed along. I am in the pushchair. It's not the time when my mother snatched an afternoon away from the new baby to dash up to the cinema at Hall Green to watch Princess Elizabeth's wedding. I'm remembering before that, to the time when there was just me. Me and my mother and her friend, Auntie Floss, who went into Solihull to the shops. The air is bright with summer. The cotton of their flowered dresses swishes at my side as we hurry, always a bit on the late side, down to catch the bus, Floss looking back over her shoulder, ready to break into a trot, waving at the driver, to show we're doing our best to get to the stop. The conductor will help to fold the pushchair. On a good day. When he doesn't, Floss will give my mother a meaning look from under the rolled brim of her hat.

They are busy once we are in the shops. Smelling of talcum, lipsticked, they compare patterns, they test out the feel of cloth between their fingers. They weigh serving dishes in their hands. They glance at each other. They shrug their shoulders. Their voices, like a song, answer each other, rising and falling, at the back of my head. My attention is not on them. It does not need to be. It is free, to spy out among the legs and the corners of counters and the hems. Hems of petticoats under summer dresses. Peeptoed shoes. Red toenails. Sandals.

When I smell the special smell of coffee, I know we must be going into Pattisons. Even today there is a fragrance, a scent that lingers around some places where coffee is served that takes me back to those bright mornings. I will be let out of the pushchair to sit up at the table too, on a wooden chair with a smooth seat and a hooped back. The waitress brings another cushion. I know that I could fall out of the back if I don't sit up, so I remember to keep still. Now they sit down too, opening handbags, reaching for cigarettes, leaning forward to get a light. They are smiling and laughing, though they keep saying that they are tired. On the table is the little silver coffee pot and my mother pours from it into two cups. I just have milk in my cup. And I choose a long eclair, like a sausage with its stripe of shiny brown icing. When I have finished it, my mother wipes my face, looking carefully, not to miss any crumbs and not to hurt me. I look back up into her eyes and see only love.

There would come a day not so far in the future when she would take me shopping on her own, to buy white gloves, when she wanted to show me off to the nuns, a summer's day when the only white gloves that she could find to fit a four year old were woollen ones that made my fingers thick and stubby. Those nuns took over her care after her own mother died when she was fourteen. But that day of the white woollen gloves and all that it threatened, threatened for both of us, was not yet. In preparing me as a four year old to give up pleasure, though she did not know it, my mother was preparing me to give up my closeness with her too.

In the garden in the afternoon I play in the tin bath that has been filled with water. Am I taking a bath or am I playing? Perhaps there is no difference in that time. I know that once I had my hair washed under the kitchen tap, held up by a firm arm, a voice laughing because it was the wrong place for washing hair, while under me yawned the deep cavern of the white porcelain sink. Afterwards I am folded into the light blue sundress, one of the two my mother's friend Auntie Mollie made for me. There are no sleeves, just a binding round the holes for the arms and a little tie at the waist to keep it done up. I am light in my clean dress, standing up straight in the garden.

Then there was the baby. He was called Michael. Do I remember saying, as she was changing him 'It's like a pink rosebud' and my mother's surprised concurrence? I think I do. Or did she remember it, with fondness? Which of us was which? Michael dribbled. He held his breath when he was angry, throwing both father and mother into panic. They blew into his protesting mouth.

Upstairs I have a set of photographs from that time. Michael and I are sitting side by side on the settee. The fawn settee in uncut moquette, with the ridges that scratched. It used to stand in the lounge, a room that my mother only used for special occasions. But we are not got up for any occasion. Michael's egg-like head looks off-duty. At any moment a dribble might escape. I have that almost jumble sale look of children after the war: hand knitting and pass-me-downs. My mother would vehemently deny that I wore anything that was not brand new in those days: let's say I looked like a child of that time, soon after the war, one who might have been photographed playing in the street.

At the sight of those photographs my mother would always exclaim: why didn't your father put you into something better? It seems a photographer – there were photographers going door to door in those hard days of the late forties – a photographer had chanced to come by one morning when our father was looking after us on his own. It hurt my father that people should have to go door to door, I know, 'to be reduced to doing that', as I heard him say. He would have opened the door to the other man and invited him in.

Seated on the settee, still today, baby Michael and myself at three years old beam up into their faces, indifferent to the camera's gaze. Across the room, out of shot, stands my father, still today. Only by taking the measure of the trust that is written in our lifted faces do I gauge my father's presence. Without this image on the slightly sticky, warping paper, I would not be able to reconstruct his presence or his children's joy and confidence in him. What happened, I ask myself today, what came between to cut me off from those feelings for my father and from the closeness with him that my brother and I once shared?

Ian Suttie and the tenderness taboo

Looking back, I am struck by how clear I was at three years old about what was going on around me, without the intermediary of words. It was not from words that I drew my information. But I am left with a question about loss. In my story I seem to stand on the brink of a precipice in time, a moment after which there followed separation, when the links with mother, father and brother were sheered away. The human world that I see before me, and on whose verge I myself stand at three years old, seems to be founded not on the taboo on incest but on forgetting and on putting an end to closeness and intimacy.

When I was sent off to school in the convent, handed over by my mother to the nuns, I learned to forget my father and how close we had been when I was small. Some might claim that in describing that cut-off I was speaking of an experience that was true only of my own situation and of the history of my own family, one which had no wider relevance beyond. Yet I myself would argue differently here. Instead I would say that my own early perception of catastrophic change spoke of an experience which is widely shared. The experience of division between fathers and daughters, brothers and sisters, mothers and children does not in itself give rise to sexual abuse. But the evidence suggests, as I will go on to argue through my chosen examples, that there are crucial links between this forced separation and the compulsive behaviour of those who perform acts of abuse. It lays a foundation for such acts.

For the moment, though, let me begin by connecting my own vision as a child with the work of Ian Suttie, the early British psychoanalyst, who in his 1935 book *The Origins of Love and Hate* identifies an early moment of loss, one accompanied by shame and confusion, which in his view is not individual or accidental but systemic. It is a moment of damage that all children sustain as they are prepared to meet the conditions of life in the outside world, according to him. Suttie was writing about the care that children receive not from bad mothers but from mothers who seem like good ones, who are meeting the regular standards of good practice. According to his disturbing argument, even children who receive what is taken to be good care from their mothers, as I did myself, from mothers who are acting in good faith, are in that very process exposed to mutilation and loss.

The name of Suttie and his work have remained known principally to therapists, in part perhaps because Suttie himself died young, a few days before the publication of his only book. Nevertheless, his thought has been very widely influential, above all in the development of the study of relations between mother and child, which is now known as object relations theory. In a sense, it was on the back of the pioneering work of Ian Suttie, which had caused a stir when it was first published that John Bowlby based his own observations, twenty years on. Suttie was one of the first to conceptualize the notion of attachment and bonding as the foundation of emotional life and to write of the mourning and deprivation that follow when those connections are broken. It was such breaks, he believed, that were responsible for giving rise to emotions of hatred, rather than any inherent tendency to evil, such as the original sin of which Christianity speaks.

Suttie's work included a dimension that Bowlby's lacked. During the First World War, as a young psychiatrist, Suttie had been posted to the Middle East, where he worked with patients from many different cultures. Suttie himself was a Scot and he did most of his work in Britain, a country which is known abroad for its harshness to children, but he supported his own observations and arguments by references gathered from his wide reading across a range of disciplines. From the start, his understanding of human behaviour also combined the perspective of an anthropologist. When he came to argue that the relationship with the mother was the most important element in establishing identity and the inner life, Suttie drew attention to the fact that this statement was at odds with the patriarchal way of thinking, which considered the child's relationship with the father to be the one which determined who it was. He saw his own work as offering a conscious challenge to the ways of thinking that had been developed under the system which put fathers first.

It was the transition between the world of home and the outside world on which Suttie focused, arguing that across the world, to a greater or lesser extent, it was standard practice for mothers to withdraw tenderness from their young children, the tenderness in which they had been raised as babies, and to do so before they were ready for it. This is not a necessary separation of the kind that we are now often urged to aim for that Suttie was describing but something more like a forced surrender, one breaking the old link between parent and child. The break does not arise spontaneously as part of human development but is brought about by mothers themselves, without realizing the implications of their action and in the belief that they are acting in the child's best interests. This practice, which he saw as universal, could only be explained, so he thought, by reference to the way that life was lived in the outside world, that is in terms of a mutilation imposed by way of adapting to that world outside.

The break which Suttie identifies as systemic comes while children are still at home, as they begin to be prepared for life in a world which is ordered differently, one in which tenderness or sensitivity to others, the awareness which has so far been the very breath of life to the child, are despised, especially tenderness between men. Out there in the public world, separation rather than intimacy rules, as he reminds his readers, noting how that world is organized around separations, a separation between women and men, between men and the world of women and children, and between generations, between parent and child.

Suttie asks his readers to look on these divisions with fresh eyes, not to view them as natural or inevitable but to recognize them as artificial, that is produced by culture, as the product of choices that have been made and as associated with giving a preferential value to men. Reflecting on Suttie's argument, it seems to me that as a young child I was already living in a place where these divisions were making themselves felt. I was still joined in feeling with my father and brother, yet in the company of my mother and her friends I already knew the separate lives that women make for themselves without the company of men. In that early moment of transition I had not yet experienced the trauma that he describes, the moment of loss when connection, inner and outer, is lost. To pinpoint that experience Suttie speaks in terms of the child's discovery that its own offers of tenderness, the reciprocity that was once so welcome, are now rejected as inadequate because something different is required. Seeing this cut-off operating world-wide, just as the taboo on incest is said to do, Suttie named it as the taboo on tenderness. Suttie argues that it is this taboo, rather than one against incest, which structures both the inner world of individuals and the outer one in which we live together in society.

Substituting tenderness as the behaviour that is forbidden throws our life as adults into a new light. The effect on the inner life of children of the violent early change which Suttie describes is

catastrophic. He writes of grief, for the loss of the original relationship with the mother, whose terms, as we know from Bowlby,
are the only ones which respect the child's own nature, and of a
rage which is nothing but appropriate. Suttie also names anxiety,
humiliation and confusion, the feelings that today are associated
with psychological trauma, though he himself does not use this
term, writing at that time. Children are without power to resist
when they are required to give up the only language of relationship that they know. The complexity of what they experience in
that moment is beyond speech. Perhaps the most lasting impression is of shame, a shame that leads them to question their own
instincts and perceptions on finding that they have made the
wrong move, that they have as it were misunderstood the rules
of the game. In Suttie's view, avoiding the memory of this early
shame, banishing it from the mind, becomes the most powerful
imperative of emotional life in adults.

The feelings around this 'violent change', as Suttie argues, are
ones that we would like to leave behind because they are so
painful, but like the fragments and shards from any traumatic
experience they keep re-presenting themselves in later life. Most
of us know what it is to writhe at the memory of social occasions
where we feel we made fools of ourselves. In those moments of
terrible embarrassment, of disproportionate shame at remembered mistakes, 'mistakes that we regret more than real crimes',
as he points out, Suttie argues that it is the old early shame
coming back to us and with a vengeance, as they say. Perhaps it
is not vengeance that these feelings want, however, though it
seems likely that they do underpin much popular enthusiasm for
punishment, so much as recognition, to be taken back and
reintegrated into our understanding of the past.

But according to Suttie, there is a huge resistance against going
back, against revisiting the world that we once knew, now that
the flaming sword of shame stands at its gate. In consequence
that taboo on tenderness which is inflicted on us when we are
very young continues to freeze our stance as adults. Suttie speaks
of its manifestation in the adult as a refusal to participate in the
emotion of others, in case painful longings are aroused, a refusal
that may have the effect of cruelty and which he names as 'psychological blindness'. One of the most obvious manifestations of
that blindness, I would argue myself, is our common blindness to
the prevalence of incest and to the emotional conditions which

give rise to it. Under patriarchy, the social organization that puts a premium on forms of behaviour that it identifies with men, psychological blindness and the cruelty which that entails characterize what is understood as the grown-up way of being in the world.

With these arguments, Suttie consciously makes a break with Freud and with his model of the process by which the human psyche develops. Looking back, as John Bowlby would write, fifty years later the moment could be clearly seen as an epistemological break. Yet it is only today, in seeking to overcome our ignorance concerning incest and abuse, that the full explanatory power of the tenderness taboo as he named it can be realized. Remembering this concept and the dangers that follow on attributing special qualities to men, remembering too the child's early pleasure in those it loves, we can go forward to harmonize features of the debate around incest which up till now have remained discordant and contradictory.

Mystification

There has been a tendency, one not confined to western writers, to take the attitude that incest involves exploring pleasures that are both delicious and unreasonably forbidden, pleasures that are secret and unfamiliar. Enthusiasm for the sexual pleasure to be had from children was reported in a 1997 study compiled by UNICEF in Pakistan, while it was in the name of pleasure that some western magazines for men have championed the right of fathers and daughters to have sex. These views have not been confined to the ignorant and uninformed; Robin Fox, the anthropologist, once went so far as to imply that girls would probably enjoy the experience of sleeping with their fathers if only those in authority did not spoil it for them.

At this some readers might be tempted simply to withdraw in alarm, but it seems to me that we would do better to hold our ground, remembering Suttie and the fierce suppression of the longing for intimacy that he described. That might prompt us to ask about psychological blindness, the blindness to the needs of children that such statements reveal. Pleasure and blindness seem fused in the minds of these speakers almost as if they were one and the same thing, or as if, perhaps, there had been a moment in the past when it became safer, less painful, not to remember about love, a moment when intelligence stalled. Public voices, with their appearance of impersonal authority, sometimes reinforce this confusion: in Britain on 6 January 1999 the *Guardian* newspaper saw fit to print an obituary of Petra Tegetmeier, the daughter of Eric Gill, the British artist who made a practice of abusing his young daughters, in which he was endorsed for 'initiating them into the mysteries of sex'. It took a woman reader to write in offering a different language, with a letter that objected 'I thought that it was called child abuse.'

Mystification has tried to make something sacred out of a blindness which occurs in the context of incest. The most famous theory of the place of the incest taboo in our inner lives was the work of Sigmund Freud, who illustrated it by appropriating the ancient story of Oedipus, the man who slept with his own mother. It is a long story, involving riddles and mysteries, but a simple outline will do to remind us here: Oedipus was abandoned as a baby, after an oracle warned his parents of what would come to pass, that he would grow up to kill his father and marry his mother. When he realized, as an adult, what he had done, he put out his own eyes. In a way, the close is the strangest part of the story: why did he do that, I remember asking, on hearing it for the first time as a child.

When Oedipus blinds himself in that story, we ourselves might wonder today about mutilation: doctors get concerned nowadays about people who self-harm. His gesture has usually been taken, however, as appropriate and as an expression of shame, a message that seems to come to us with all the authority of classical learning backed up by the weight of Freud's own genius. Yet what reader can fail to notice that the ancient story, like Suttie's own observations, makes links between shame and choosing not to see, between shame and intimacy with a mother? Both appear to be describing the same inner world.

Freud situated the taboo on incest at the centre of individual emotional life and made it the hinge of human development as well as the ground of civilization itself. The Oedipus complex, as he named it, was the process by which the inner drives, which he claimed were originally in conflict, became organized and properly ordered so that the basis for a moral and responsible human consciousness could be laid down. It is a theory that now seems like second nature to many people, a premise, a starting point for thinking. For that reason alone, our argument needs to take it in. But one problem with Freud's theory, as Ian Suttie observed, was that it meant supposing young children naturally passed through a state of violent inner conflict which was not always successfully 'worked through'. Remembering Darwin, Suttie wrote 'I would require a good deal of evidence to believe that any successful species can be born with useless and even self-conflicting dispositions.'

To understand how Oedipus with his violent story came to be taken as the prototype for normal human development we need to begin with the story of Freud himself. At the beginning of his career it was sexual abuse and its consequences that demanded his attention. Freud, who was working in Vienna, from the last years of the nineteenth century, started out by believing the stories that his women patients told him about the abuse they had experienced, but the implications of that discovery were too much for him. They would have woken such a storm if he had attempted to open people's eyes in that place and at that time that he withdrew from his original theory concerning sexual abuse and instead described what his patients had told him as fantasy. His new theory claimed that children desired sexual contact with the other-sex parent but that they had to learn to repress this longing: that is how he came to put the taboo on incest at the centre of individual emotional life.

In place of amplifying what these women had told him about abuse, Freud constructed a theory that focused on men and on the danger of men getting too close to their mothers. He based his argument on the need to produce men, for it was on the separation between mothers and sons, so he explained, that the ordering of human society depended. Without that separation, moral and responsible human consciousness could not be developed in men, the consciousness, or mindset as we should call it, that he claimed was the foundation of 'civilized' life. Today, we might well agree with him that a special way of thinking that is passed down between men lies behind the organization of our world, though we might be less sure, seeing the impact we have made on the planet, that we wanted that way of thinking to continue. At this point, like Ian Suttie, I choose to move away from Freud. In taking education as my starting point for thinking about incest, I connect trauma and abuse with the ideal of masculinity and with the mindset that is passed on to girls and boys in its name.

Though he believed that women were also subject to the incest taboo, Freud claimed that he did not understand their inner lives: in spite of all they had told him, he insisted that women were a 'dark continent' for him, like Africa. Claiming to speak in the voice of reason, instead Freud offers, by his behaviour, an example of obedience and orthodoxy. He names the separation between women and men which is such a salient feature of social organization as we know it. Today, the study of gender has put that separation into question, but as a man of his time Freud was in no position to make that move and instead he takes separation as a necessary principle. In arriving at his theory indeed, Freud himself does what he claims every man must do and moves away from women: over-riding what his patients had told him and reinterpreting their evidence, he repudiates the women he has been close to, the women who told him about their experience of abuse. Actively maintaining the distance between women and men, Freud pretends not to know.

Though we might ourselves be tempted to speak about mirages, it was in the story of Oedipus that Freud thought that he saw the incest taboo in embodied form: like the name of Oedipus, this story has come to be equated in western thought with the taboo. But it would make sense to go back to the original story, as it was before Freud made it the symbol of his theory in order to read it afresh. Today, in order to ask about incest, I have chosen to take a new tack and to adopt the point of view of the child. What happens to the story of Oedipus, let us ask ourselves, how does its meaning change when we put the experience of the child rather than that of the adult at its centre?

Then the fact that as an infant Oedipus was abandoned and raised by strangers takes its full weight. As a theorist, Suttie spoke of the loss of early tenderness between parent and child, a loss of which this story also speaks, linking it, as appeared in my own past, with religious authority. Read in the light of his observations, this story tells of the child abandoned by his parents following the instructions of a voice that they believed it would be impious to challenge, when an oracle gives them a divine warning. This child, from whom tenderness is withdrawn, so that it seems his original parents have disappeared and he is being raised by strangers, is filled with rage and shame by that loss, a rage and shame that as a man he cannot bear to know. Once he becomes an adult, this child's only desire is to avenge himself on his father and to restore the old intimacy with his mother, but this time around, on adult terms and preserving his new dignity as a man, by becoming her lover.

This old story comes from ancient Greece, where the European ideal of democracy first took shape. But like the story of the

Emperor's new clothes, this story appears to be one that invites a more sceptical look at the symbols we have been taught to respect: read from this angle, the story of Oedipus is telling unwelcome truths about the violence that is brought into the world by parents who are well-meaning and morally responsible, parents who are acting for the best. Like Ian Suttie, the doctor writing in the twentieth century, this ancient story diagnosed a sickness in the community, speaking of children abandoned for what seem to be the best of reasons, children who learn a shame which makes them choose not to see. Both therapist and folk-tale point to a world in which there is a cut-off to closeness between parents and children which undermines later attempts at intimacy. Rather than a taboo on incest, at the centre of this world stands a taboo on knowing, both on the knowing that comes from closeness with another person and on the knowing that depends on using your own eyes. Rather than democracy, it appears that shame and this taboo on knowing are a time-honoured foundation of the western way of life.

Social institutions

Many arguments that do not stand up are put forward in the context of the incest taboo. This means picking out those that do carry some weight before we can go on. The world of psychology and psychoanalysis is not the only one to give precedence to a set of ideas which go by the name of the incest taboo. Among other intellectual disciplines too there seems to be a general acceptance that the taboo on incest is important, even central to the forms of social organization and to civilization itself, yet unanimity and even logic break down right after that point. It is agreed that 'the taboo on incest' supports the way we live our everyday lives and that our institutions, which are designed to protect the life of the community, the institutions of religion, family and state, depend for their survival on the maintenance of this taboo. This makes it all the more remarkable that there is so much uncertainty and contradiction surrounding it.

We may ask whether our institutions bring as much danger as they do protection. To start with the scientific argument: like many others of my generation I myself grew up under the impression that sex between blood relatives needs at all costs to be forbidden on medical grounds. It was often repeated that such unions were likely to produce monsters. Geneticists do warn us today that there may be risks if a child is born to parents who are very closely related genetically. But there is no sacred mystery underpinning this warning: it refers to limited risks that are now calculable.

If both parents bear the same genetic code, when that code is one that makes them carriers either of a disease or of a predisposition to one, the odds are increased and it becomes much more likely that their child will in fact develop the disease in question. This warning has nothing to do with matters of morals, for if only one parent is a carrier, the child is not any more at risk than if it were the offspring of parents who were not related to each other.

Though it has been rediscovered by the science of our own day, this appears to have been known for over two hundred years. From the beginning of the nineteenth century breeders of stock animals were discounting the so-called dangers of inbreeding and soon they were routinely arguing, on the basis of experience, that persistent inbreeding was the more reliable way to fix desirable characteristics and of getting them to breed true. That was how the pioneers of stock breeding had begun, in the eighteenth century. 'Mate sire to daughter and son to dam' urged the 1897 volume *How to Choose a Dog and How to Select a Puppy*. All that mattered was avoiding a common predisposition to disease. These breeders were quite aware that they were defying an 'extraordinary fear' of such unions that was widespread but they set such notions aside as 'ignorance' and 'delusion'. As we know, that ignorance and delusion continue to survive and it appears that they are not fortuitous but play a central role in social organization. Yet they also direct us towards the question of fear, a fear that is out of the ordinary, to the role of this fear in suppressing understanding and to the threat of punishment. These are forces that later on in my argument we will repeatedly observe at work in maintaining the confusion around sexual abuse.

You might think that it would be a step towards clarification to invoke the law and to point out that under the law incest is forbidden, and so it is, but laws differ from one society to another, according to their history, and even from one state to another in the United States. There is no universally agreed definition of incest: it simply means sexual union between people who are linked by connections of a kind that in their own particular society would ban them from marriage.

The connections that are named and forbidden under pain of punishment in the name of incest are not constant between one culture and another and can even appear counter-intuitive. In the book of Leviticus, where every degree of forbidden contact is enumerated, there is nothing to say directly that a man is banned from sleeping with his own daughter. On the other hand it is notorious that under English law in the nineteenth century a man was not permitted to marry the sister of his deceased wife. It would be easy to spend time in showing how much variation there is between one society and another in the relationships that are designated as incestuous and therefore incur punishment, but that might turn out to be another distraction. It might make better sense to concentrate on a few landmarks, for in all the mass of curious and contradictory examples that anthropological studies of incest have to offer there are still certain landmarks that can be made out.

Anthropologists offer a way to make sense of the multiple forms that forbidden relationships may take when they point out that the incest taboo is about controlling whom people may marry. For them it can be explained in terms of what they call exogamy, that is in terms of the need to marry 'out' in order to facilitate the circulation of wealth and resources in the interests of the community's survival, which depends on prosperity and trade. It seems likely to me, however, that other interests too are at stake. When they link incest with marriage, anthropologists link it with an institution which, like the laws against incest, also takes many different forms across the world, the institution which has been set up to regulate intimacy between women and men and to define the terms under which it should occur.

As an institution, marriage has symbolized the relationship between all women and all men, marking the separation between these groups, in the different rights and duties traditionally assigned to women and to men within marriage. Not all cultures have made that separation so rigorous as the institution of Christian marriage. The example of ancient Egypt is often cited in discussions of incest, for the Egyptians permitted marriages that are forbidden today in Europe and America. In Egypt unions between brother and sister were allowed. The parents of Cleopatra, the last pharaoh of Egypt, were sister and brother but such marriages were not permitted only to members of the royal house. Even at the time when the Romans, whose traditions were quite different and from whom we derive many of our own current attitudes, had taken control of Egypt, during the first century CE, marriages between sister and brother appear to have made up a quarter of all marriages in the area known as the Fayoum.

It seems reasonable to connect this with the fact that in Egypt brother and sister were treated more equally under the law than they were anywhere else in the ancient world. Creating men, the task that Freud saw was so important, and in which assigning special rights to men is a central feature, is a high-maintenance activity, one that is liable to be undermined by letting women and men find out how much they have in common with each other. When western cultures forbid siblings to marry, it may be on the grounds that they already know themselves to be so close as children of the same parents that anything closer would put the general separation between the sexes that is enforced at risk. But in Egypt, where there was not the same drive to keep up any such marked and artificial separation, there was equally no need to forbid such marriages.

There are good reasons to be against abuse, or against bearing children who may be genetically at risk, but these reasons do not seem to be what lies behind the intense public hostility to 'incest' as an offence. As a crime, a contravention of public law, 'incest' inspires a horror that also seems artificial and moreover open to manipulation. What has been seen as lawful and appropriate in choice of partner, not subject to taboo as 'incest', varies so much that it leads me to wonder whether an attempt simply to secure obedience, to secure it as an end in itself, lies at the root of the legislation around incest that is found in all societies. Laws that are manifestly so arbitrary, yet reach so intimately into the workings of desire in individual lives, look to me like an attempt to make obedience more salient to the mind than passion, to crush out independence and spontaneity. When priestly castes in ninth-century Persia encouraged men to take their daughters and nieces, even on occasion their own mothers, as their wives, they did it on the grounds that it was the best way to maintain a harmonious household. It would be easy to see this recommendation only as a bid for domestic peace, but that might be a mistake. By assuming that the mothers themselves, let alone the other women, would have no say in the matter, it rests its notion of harmony on silencing all voices except that of the priest.

Religion has always been closely associated with the ban on
'incest'. Naming those who may or may not be married has
usually been done in the name of religion, of the sacred and what
is holy, though it has not always been so apparent as it is today
that the sacred object in whose defence this taboo is constructed
is the idea of manhood and of masculinity as a separate form of
human life. It was in 1949 that the French anthropologist Claude
Lévi-Strauss opened his study, *The Elementary Structures of Kinship*,
by acknowledging the link with religion and by noting its continuing power. 'Few social prescriptions in our society have so kept that
aura of respectful fear which clings to sacred objects', he wrote.

But when he went on to make links between religion and
political organization, between racial hatred and the incest taboo,
between family structures and the forms taken by behaviour
outside the home, Lévi-Strauss opened out a debate which had
seemed closed. He converted the generalized observation that
the incest taboo supports all social structures into a set of specific
connections which were both unexpected and disturbing. Lévi-
Strauss observed that certain communities punish those who defy
bans on inter-racial marriage just exactly as they do those who
are found to be guilty of incest:

> Significantly, . . . incest proper, and its metaphorical form as the
> violation of a minor (by someone 'old enough to be her father', as
> the expression goes), even combines in some countries with its
> direct opposite, inter-racial sexual relations, an extreme form of
> exogamy, as the two most powerful inducements to horror and
> collective vengeance.

Confronted with this parallel, one that could not have been pre-
dicted by means of logic, Lévi-Strauss moves over to reading
metaphorically. He suggests that even when sexual abuse occurs
outside families, it would make sense to see it as motivated by
impulses that can be traced back to the forms of family organization. These forms, as I would argue, separate out one member
from another along the lines of gender in the interests of maintaining the special dignity of men. In offering his reminder of the
metaphorical importance of fathers, Lévi-Strauss invites us to
think about the predicament in which this separation from women
leaves men and to ask why a man should seek to close the gap
between himself and others, particularly to close the gap between

himself and a young girl. Such considerations shape the view that I am putting forward.

In making the link with race Lévi-Strauss offers another new point of departure for thinking about this taboo. Following his observation I have concluded that there is no comprehending this issue without also confronting the question of race. Lévi-Strauss associates incest with politics and with a sustained attempt to secure a society whose members are constrained, humiliated and divided when he compares the taboo on incest with bans on inter-racial sex. That makes the self-righteous horror and vengeance that are inspired when the ban on incest is contravened more open to question. As he points out, those are the very emotions that inspired past lynchings of American blacks.

We may be used to borrowing the language of anthropology ourselves and to thinking of 'incest' as 'a taboo' but we don't always remember that any taboo is also a prohibition against speaking. Naming something as taboo implies that it is to be avoided even in discussion: the object of taboo is placed beyond the reach of language. Perhaps it is not surprising that in setting out to write about incest I find that I am met with looks of incomprehension or distaste. And yet, if we look into its history, as recorded in the *Oxford English Dictionary*, the word 'taboo' itself and the moment when it was picked up in Polynesia by Captain James Cook at the end of the eighteenth century mark an opening, the breaking of a long silence. After that it became possible to name taboo as an institution and to recognize it as one used to regulate society, like the institution of marriage or like the church. Once the practice was named and identified, the word was picked up by others too. As the *Dictionary* itself records, the new word began to be used by British writers in naming their own experience at home.

According to the *Dictionary*, the institution of taboo was usually controlled by the king or great chiefs in conjunction with the priests. It meant that an object or person was:

Set apart for or consecrated to a special use or purpose; restricted to the use of a god, a king, priests, or chiefs, while forbidden to general use; prohibited to a particular class (esp. to women), or to a particular person or persons; inviolable, sacred; forbidden, unlawful; also said of persons under a perpetual or temporary prohibition from certain actions, from food, or from contact with others.

Until that date in 1777 when Cook made a note of the word
'tapu' in Tonga, there had been no language to name the process
by which authority for a select group was manufactured and
obedience on the part of the community was obtained. While in
Polynesia, he and his companions observed, as they might never
have remarked on it at home, the part that was played by the
institution of taboo in creating the social order that surrounded
them. That order, which separated chiefs and priests from the
mass of the people and divided women from men, was so familiar to them, since it corresponded with what they knew at home,
that they took it for granted, just as the compilers of the *Oxford
English Dictionary* and many others seem to do today.

The notion of taboo forced itself on Cook's attention because
it went against all his own instincts of fellow-feeling and kept
people apart:

> Not one of them would sit down, or eat a bit of anything . . . On
> expressing my surprise at this, they were all *taboo*, as they said;
> which word has a very comprehensive meaning; but, in general,
> signifies that a thing is forbidden. Why they were laid under such
> restraints, at present, was not explained.

This absence of explanation, which Cook also noted, was a more
important part of the proceedings than he could have known.
Temporary taboos were often imposed quite arbitrarily, so that
it was impossible to make any particular sense of them. Putting
ourselves in that place, it is clear how taboo made the world
unpredictable, so that however careful they were a person might
find themselves suddenly in the wrong. Something did not have
to be important or even dangerous to be declared taboo. It seems
obvious that the exercise was one in social control, intending to
shut down independence of mind and spontaneous action and
instead to substitute obedience, particularly in women as the
class most subject to taboo.

Cook came to this conclusion for himself, watching what happened after a taboo had been broken. Infringing a taboo meant
becoming taboo oneself, that is ostracized and cut off from the
rest of the community, just as that brother and sister in Michigan
were cut off when they were sent to jail. There were degrees
in ostracism, but total ostracism in Tonga and in some other
societies too was a punishment that could mean a slow death, if
no steps were taken to show remorse for what had been done.

However, there was an easy way out: 'When the *taboo* is incurred, by paying obeisance to a great personage, it is thus easily washed off.' An act of ritual obedience, a public embrace of the vision which claimed that some men were more worthy than others and that women were separate from men, was all that was required.

It would be nice to believe that the social institutions which taboo is directed at preserving were ones that made life safe for the community but the evidence seems to point to something else. In working to silence questions in the interests of keeping an ancient order of authority unchanged, taboo actively brings about harm. It causes damage to members of the community at every level by impairing the ability to reflect on experience and to put what they know into practice.

Danger

Being close to a mother may well put children at risk, if not exactly for the reasons offered by Freud. In a world that is governed by the system of taboo, as women, all mothers take their place in the group that is most at risk of being found guilty and is most liable to punishment. So far as they have internalized this threat, rather than resisting it, mothers pass their own fear and shame on to their children as part of the culture and the world view that they transmit. The voice of childhood tells me that I myself knew this even when I was very small:

> I am in a car. It is very hot. The doors are shut. I look through the window. Mrs Hathaway has gone into the house.

As I recapture this voice it takes me back to the sense of a mind that is pristine. I know that my mother's friend, Mrs Hathaway, does not come back soon, though the visit she is paying is much shorter than she expected it to be. Inside the house is Mrs Hathaway's mother. I liked pretty Mrs Hathaway and I had no reason to be afraid of her mother or of any other stranger, sheltered as I was in those days. But when Mrs Hathaway stopped her car and told me that we were going to get out and go inside to see her mother, a door seemed to open inside me and something huge and terrible poured in. Nowadays I should say that I sensed danger, a threat of being flooded by feelings that did not originate in myself. I was stoical as a small child, not given to panics, or so my mother would tell me later – 'You stood still with your back full of thorns from the rosebush that you'd fallen into and you never made a sound as your father and I picked them out' – but for once, I raised my voice aloud and wept. I wept loudly and I would not stop, I would not listen. In the end, Mrs Hathaway gave up and went in to visit her mother on her own.

In the fifty years that have passed since that afternoon, I've never lost the sense of the power of my own refusal, though I have puzzled to understand what prompted it. But now that I'm beginning to wonder about what is truly dangerous to children, I think that I begin to comprehend. There is a form of resistance that is not just healthy but vital and necessary to survival. 'No', says my two-year-old granddaughter, laughing, wagging her finger in the mirror and glancing back at me. By her game, Nina is showing me that she can defend herself against me. Looking back at myself, at her age, from the vantage point of today, I see another child who could defend herself, a child who had also learned to do this because she had been cared for with respect. By three years old my mother's care had given me wisdom, the wisdom of the body, so that I knew enough to protect myself against danger, and could shut off the fear that already dwelled in my mother and was threatening to invade my own life.

At three years old I had no words for this knowledge. It was in the form of images that I recognized what I knew, just as today, when I look back at the image of that child sitting alone by herself, shut up in the hot car, I understand that she had shut herself away. At three years old, when I found myself cast, as it were, in a scene that would involve a mother, the fact that I already sensed fear in my own mother leapt into life, as if it had been projected upon a screen. But when language came into the picture and my mother's fears began to take on the form of stories, the stories that she passed on to me in the name of religious teaching, I could no longer keep myself apart and they poured in at my open ears.

In this next phase of my argument I move on to ask about parents and danger, first comparing my own experience with the picture of family life offered by Louis Malle in his movie *Murmur of the Heart*. There Malle shows a mother who refuses to pass on shame. It is the father who maintains tradition by remaining emotionally distant from his wife and sons. Malle invites us to recognize something familiar in the world which he represents: it is one from which fathers are emotionally absent while being represented in the lives of their children by priests. This move on my part marks the first step in a gradual approach to real-life cases of abuse. The stories of film-maker Jennifer Montgomery and the writer Sappho Durrell follow, leading up to the case of a father who proved to be extremely dangerous, Father James Porter, the Catholic priest who was charged with sexual abuse in Massachusetts.

It is closeness between father and daughter that most people would associate with danger. My own experience as a woman, however, suggests something different, something that is more complicated. In my own case, it was separation from each of my parents and from a sense of who they were in themselves, a process that took place over the course of my education as a girl, which was dangerous, placing me psychologically at risk. Those separations, to which I suspect my classmates were also sub-jected within the particular terms of their own lives, led me to make blind misreadings of the world.

'Why are you writing this book?', a friend pressed me one day. At the time when the question was put to me I was surprised, even mildly affronted, but I could make no reply. I did not recognize that I was struggling against something in myself. Only when I asked myself whether there were any experiences of my own that could not be spoken of did I begin to understand. I knew that there had been a single incident, a moment of shock and withdrawal, for which I had never found language. I will come to that story in a little while. But before I could get to grips with that moment, with the blank I had discovered in myself, I was overtaken by a reminder from much earlier in my life, a flashback from the time when I was very small.

I was sitting up in bed one night, reading, waiting for my husband to finish brushing his teeth and come to join me, when I felt again, without any warning, a flood of sensations that I had experienced once before. This time, as they passed through me, I could put a name to the wave of pure helplessness followed by panic and a weightless sense of disorientation. Simultaneously, I knew, instinctively and without effort, where those feelings came from, as though they had been hibernating inside me, waiting for the moment to emerge and be recognized, waiting since a day when I was five or six years old.

It was about the time when I was first going to school that my Irish mother had instructed me in the doctrine of Hell. Thinking back, I imagine that she was trying to give me a head start with the nuns. Their approval became all that she had to cling to after her own mother died when she was aged fourteen. But she had to stifle something in herself in order to speak of Hell to me at four years old. The most intuitive of women, she must have had to steel herself against the agitation in me which her words were causing and which she could not have failed to pick up. 'Hell is the place where the wicked burn in flames for all eternity', she explained. If I was overwhelmed by hearing this, it was not because I immediately feared such punishment, though it would be easy to attribute that to a child. Checking back through those emotions from the past, so pristine on their return to me, I find something else. I find a child who was shattered to discover that her own sense of reality had been trumped.

Up till that moment, like other children, I had been piecing the world together step by step and rooting myself in it as I went. Now, with a force that shocked me, I found that there was another story, one that I had never suspected and that this was the real one, the one that overrode everything I thought I knew. Finding my own explorations redundant, for it seemed as if they had failed me, I felt as though the ground had been snatched from under my feet.

Yet as a child I was loved and well cared for: every night before I fell asleep my mother would sit by my bed and read to me. The habit only came to an end, she would remind me wryly, when she found that underneath the bedclothes I was reading something else. I think that I did manage somehow to keep another sense of reality alive in myself as I was growing up, one that was different, but with it now there was also hidden, concealed even from myself, a fury as overwhelming as my sense of shock.

That rage surfaced separately in a second flashback. Perhaps not entirely by chance, it erupted in Mexico, where the priests once claimed that only the hearts of living victims would satisfy the gods. Tense with apprehension, for I had broken my ankle a year or two previously on a slope, I was picking my way down a steep flight of temple steps, early one morning, steps slippery today only with dew, when my anxious concentration was broken by a shout. It was the familiar voice of my husband. 'You're OK', he yelled. 'We've got the ambulance waiting for you.'

My knees had already taken on a life of their own, quivering away. Now I came to a halt, paralysed. According to Amnesty International, sudden blasts of noise are one way of breaking people down, though of course I did not know this at the time when my mother's voice broke in on my inner world. But today when I heard my husband's voice intrude on me, speaking in riddles, I was flooded with energy. It was as if my whole body were remembering. Trained now, by all the theatre classes I have taken in the last few years, my body amplified my fury and I found my full voice. Into the echoing space between the ancient ruins, where the early tourist groups were massing, I spoke.

First I swore at him. Then, 'Get away from me with your senseless bellowing, I was terrified already.' I felt as though I were expanding, as if I were on a stage and it was my job to let the obscene gestures I was making with my fingers and my voice of disrespect fill all the space. I allowed my face to become a mask of hatred. In my passion I lost all other concerns, least of all for whether my husband would ever speak to me again. A minute later though, with his arm around my shoulders, he was explaining that he had meant to encourage me. 'I didn't realize how frightened you were', he said. How could he have realized, when I was so incompletely aware myself of what had been set resonating in me by that place?

When it is ready, as Cathy Caruth argues in *Unclaimed Experience*, her book on memory and trauma, the mind takes us back to what we really know. In common with others who write on trauma, Caruth describes flashback as a symptom, one which indicates the fact that damage to the mind has been sustained some time before. Like cognition, with which it is closely associated, trauma is what doctors call a whole body event. At the moment of psychological trauma, the mind is lost, that is the ability to know and to comprehend what is happening fails. Under the strain of attempting to absorb experience that it cannot assimilate or organize, the whole system becomes overwhelmed and goes down. In its aftermath there exists neurological damage that can be measured, as Judith Herman indicates in the afterword to the 2000 edition of her book *Father–Daughter Incest*. This damage also shows itself in the form that memories take. They arrive long afterwards, only in the form of flashbacks and isolated images as though the experience itself, rather than the nervous system, had been broken into fragments.

But Caruth places her own emphasis on the inner drive to restoration and repair that these memories reveal. They make it possible
to retrieve not only a knowledge that is more intact but also the
voice, the voice that becomes lost under trauma at the same time
as the ability to comprehend. Bessell van der Kolk, who has written
widely on trauma, reports that it is the failure of their own voices
that causes the greatest distress and shame to trauma sufferers,
whether they are veterans of war or survivors of sexual abuse.

My own experience of flashback, however, did not occur in
connection with such events. Instead it was associated with something that is usually taken to be wholesome, with the teaching
that is given at a mother's knee. When this teaching took the
form of a warning concerning the consequences of offending a
father who lived in heaven, it ran counter to what I already
knew, knew about my own father and about unconditional love.
But I was also aware of my father's temper. 'Why is my father so
angry?' was the unspoken question of my childhood.

At that time I was not yet equal to the task of separating
reality from myth. Nowadays it is a different story, however.
Today that drive to restoration and repair of which Caruth speaks
prompts me as I write. I have always known that there was one
episode, one fragment of my adolescence about which I had
remained silent. At the time the experience was overwhelming
and I only longed for escape: later I had no means of making
sense of it. It is in such language that people describe the experience of abuse. But my own experience did not involve an encounter with another person: it was in the act of reading that as
a young girl I came face to face with a ban against seeing, an
inexplicable refusal and stalling on the part of my own mind.
Now I view it as a moment when the change that was imposed
on me in childhood, the failure of understanding that accompanied a break in relationship, was compounded and reinforced.

When I wrote an account of my growing up, as I did a few
years ago, putting together all that I could recall in the form of a
memoir, that moment of inward stalling was a piece which I was
not able to fit in. But today that missing piece looks to me like a
key, a key to my own life as a woman, one that I let fall forty years
ago, when I was a girl in school. In those days I had just lost my
mother, that is she had had the first in a series of breakdowns.
Now the Hell she had spoken of had really come to pass: for
hours she would sit staring blankly, a cigarette burning away in

her hand, rousing herself only to go to Mass. At first I raged at her in my terror but I could not hold her attention or force her back into being the mother I had known. Rather than mourning for what I had lost in her – perhaps even recognizing a warning – I had chosen to bury myself, to hide myself away as it were in my work in school. It was that girl who took herself to the library one Saturday afternoon.

When I sat down to read the play *Woman in a Dressing-Gown*, it was in the Junior Section of our little local branch library. Not that I was choosing my reading from its narrow shelves any longer, although they had once held such magic for me. I was – what age? Fourteen seems a little too old, thirteen too young. Let's say I was between thirteen and fourteen the day that I picked up a copy of the new play *Woman in a Dressing-Gown* that I had already seen discussed in the newspapers. I carried it out of the Adult Section where I had found it and bore it away to the recesses of the Children's Library.

There the books were firmly divided and categorized: 'Fiction or non-fiction?' That was all the librarian used to inquire of us children as she stamped our tickets. That day when I was thirteen, if you'd asked me why I went back to the Children's Library, I'd have said it was so that I could sit myself down to read at the big table there, but now I think differently. I see an impulse that took me back into an earlier setting, where it was clear what belonged in the category of fiction.

In those days of early adolescence, I was confused. It was not long since I had started at my senior school, St Paul's Grammar School for Girls, where I was already winning prizes. When I sat down alone to read to myself in that place where fiction and non-fiction were so strictly divided and there was no muddling up of fact and fantasy as there was in the world of my education, and in the mind of my own mother, it seems to me that I was making an attempt to turn the clock back.

At school I was becoming an expert in knowing what they wanted me to know and in beliefs that are orthodox. Yet as a young teenager, instead of the prizes I was winning, at a deeper level, under the bedclothes as it were, I suspect that I was driven by a blind wish to find something else. When I sat down to study that script, I think that I wanted to interpret life for myself, to get back a grip on my own experience and what it told me, the grip that I once had in the days when I could keep out of danger because I knew about love. When they are rising fourteen girls are curious about love.

But when I tried to go back it was a bit like being unable to stop swallowing poison. As I read, a terrible shapeless pain invaded me. That is what I remember, the moment when what I knew and what I did not want to know became fused. Perhaps it was in the face of the reminders, the painful longings that were roused in me, that I felt myself go blank. I seemed to be reading about my own mother, about my mother's life with my father but also about her life with me. The play shows a woman of middle age, a long-married woman, who has, as they say, let herself go. Or has been driven crazy by the life she's been asked to live, as a woman; that is how I would put it myself today in my own middle age. But then, at thirteen, I saw, in the shabby, disintegrating figure that is presented by the play, the unwashed woman who spent the whole day in her dressing-gown, the image of my own mother.

And as I went on reading, the shapeless horror in my heart, the feeling that could not be named or spoken, continued to spread, till the cavity of my chest was choked with it, for the husband in the play has met someone else, someone pretty and young and smart, at the place where he works. His wife finds out, or he tells her and she does not realize she's beaten, she doesn't see how far gone she is, how far from anything but pity she has travelled. She tries to smarten herself up, to make herself attractive to him. I wanted to put down the book. I wanted to scream 'Stop. Don't try. Don't offer. Save your dignity somehow.' Was I addressing these words to my mother or to myself? I stifled the voice that would have reached out to her and I turned away.

At that moment I knew nothing of my own anger against the mother who must have seemed to be abandoning me for a second time, or of any wish in myself to see her punished, though at the grammar school we had all learned to believe in punishment. I did not ask whether the shame that I was feeling was on account of my mother's behaviour or of my own stepping away from her, I felt only that something in me curdled with shame. But at thirteen I had no means of knowing that I was part of a larger pattern or that I was following a script.

From that day in the library to this I have not spoken – neither about the play I read, nor about the quaking abyss that it opened inside me, the sense of inner collapse and loss. Today I have come to ask whether I also registered in that play any truths about my father and his life, any knowledge that was brought home to me by the play. It was a question that I could not face at thirteen. I experienced such dread before what the play told me as a girl, I only wanted to escape, to stop feeling and knowing, knowing what I really felt. That involved knowing my true feelings for my father and I flinched from those. From the days when I was starting school, I had been learning to obey the will of a different father, a Father in Heaven, and to speak his language of guilt and blame, forgetting my own father and what he might want of me as his daughter. My father was a teacher: I did not recognize, in the French which was his chosen subject, his preference for the language of love.

Years later, when I was eighteen, my godmother told me that my father had met someone that he'd known before at the school where he taught and that that had played a part in my mother's collapse. What did I feel when Alice broke this to me? Let me go back: 'Your father met a lady that he used to know before, I think she was a secretary at the school. Your mother got to hear about it and that was when she had her breakdown.' It was like a brutal punch landing on a place that was already deeply bruised. If I had to put words to what I felt when I heard her, those words would be 'appalled' and 'betrayed'. As if my father, in turning to another woman, had betrayed me and what there was between us. Did I hate what Alice had to tell me because it brought home to me what I felt for him, feelings that were deeply buried or was it deeply bruised? Deeply bruised perhaps by myself in keeping them down?

I think that I picked up hope and an impulse towards life in my father, impulses that as a girl I shared with him, and that these sustained me all the time that I was growing up. But at the time when I turned away from my mother I also turned my back on the knowledge of what I meant to him. As I approached adolescence at thirteen, I was already shying away from the image of a young woman like myself in the place of my father's lover: I did not want to know what I shared with my mother and all that attracted him. I am writing a book about incest. I have to ask myself what would have happened if I had allowed myself to feel those feelings for my father that I held back and relaxed into knowing what he felt about me. Would we have become lovers?

It does not seem to me that we would. That was not my father's object: what he wanted was to claim the likeness that we shared. Once in a moment of exasperation with my mother he had said to me, 'You and I are different, Mary, we value the things of the mind.' For myself, I don't believe that I would have wanted to seduce him either. When one of his colleagues, a married man over forty, who had come to visit me in college, put his arm around me as we sat in his car and told me that he wanted to spend the afternoon lying with me in a field, I recoiled. That was not the way that I wanted to learn about love.

When we were both girls of fifteen and my French exchange Michèle put her head on his shoulder, my father asked, 'Why can't you be like this, Mary?' At his question I stood speechless, cut to the heart. Now it seems to me that he was calling me to move forward, carrying with me into the present the trust and closeness with him that I had known as a young child. But at the time I only knew that I was angry, feeling that he understood nothing about my life. Didn't he know that I had been made to change, that I was not a little girl any more? That I had changed in order to suit him, as I bitterly felt, and that I was now stuck? Stuck in a trackless waste, so that I could not go forward.

Today I look back at those games of table tennis that we played against each other, my father and myself, all that summer before I turned fourteen, my father coaching me, and at the same time doing his best to win, and I think I see what he was offering. He was showing me about himself, as a man, sharing his response with me, in the same way as my little granddaughter showed me about herself, by a game.

My father was a very keen tennis player and he wanted me to play well too. When he taught me to play as well as I could, to play as well as he did, to match him in this game at which he excelled, my father was teaching me about love. Questions of his guilt or innocence, painful as they are in view of what happened to my mother, don't seem so important to me now. If I had been able to connect those lessons with the passionate longing that I was suppressing, the longing for my lost closeness with my father that I had when I was a small child, then I would have known what it was to feel love as a grown woman. I would have had a compass in the world.

Instead, at twenty-one I chose to marry a man who had not roused those deep feelings but allowed my passionate longing to remain untouched. He too seems to have been blind to feeling, for he did not know me any more than I knew him. That old childlike longing, which had never been connected up to my adult life, finally burst forth once I admitted to myself that the marriage had been a mistake. Flooding into my life at that time, it carried me into an affair with a married man, one that ended in catastrophe, not only for myself but for my two young daughters.

I suppose there might be some who would argue that it was better, safer for me as a daughter to have been so blind, not knowing my own heart and keeping an emotional distance from my father. Looking back at my own life, at my own choices as a woman, I can only wonder: what could have been more dangerous both for me and for my own daughters than that blindness?

Louis Malle:
Murmur of the Heart

Looking back on the way my mind was trained as a girl, I find that it was structured not by a taboo on incest but by separation and by psychological resistance. Losing the difference between pain and pleasure, I learned to turn away from what I knew and from those whom I most deeply loved. Yet the attempt to switch what I knew about my father with what I was taught in the name of fathers in general was a failure. Something in me, a mind of my own, refused to forget. When Louis Malle, the film-maker, chose to look at the process by which in France a boy is educated for manhood, he saw a symmetrical invitation to turn away. But in the story of a boy of fourteen at the time of adolescence told by Malle, in his film *Murmur of the Heart*, that treacherous invitation is disarmed. It is the life in the boy's own mother and the way that they have remained close which afford him protection. In *Murmur of the Heart*, Louis Malle weighs the danger for a young boy of separation from his mother against the danger of an intimacy with her that does actually tip over into an act of incest.

Many people have believed that it was not good for boys to be allowed to stay close to their mothers. By long custom across Europe and beyond boys were taken away from their mothers and sent to be instructed by men. It has not been so frankly acknowledged in the case of girls that sending them to be instructed by women is done in order to break the link with their fathers. In *Murmur of the Heart* Malle turns a sceptical gaze on the men who are products of such isolating education and on the celibate priests who pass it on. Against them he weighs a mother and a son who have kept their closeness and who in doing so offer an implicit challenge to a whole world order and to the notion of masculinity on which it is based.

In view of what I now realize about my own debt to my father, it seems to me no accident that the mother in this film should be a woman who grew up as a girl without formal schooling, a woman who learned from the example of her own father how to live. The French have a reputation in Europe both for knowing about pleasure and for maintaining a sceptical turn of mind. Only in France, perhaps, with its tradition of anticlericalism, a resistance to the authority of the church which goes back to the time of the Revolution, could this story that Malle sets out to tell be so fully imagined and explored.

The movie which Malle himself wrote, as well as directed, sets out to explore the life of a family where there are three sons, of whom the youngest, Laurent, is just leaving childhood. In Laurent, the curiosity of the child is developing into the questioning intelligence of the adult. His mother watches as her youngest son, a boy of not more than about fourteen, begins to reach out for life on his own account: and he watches her. He sees a still young and beautiful woman, Italian, a Sophia Loren lookalike, who was married, as she tells him herself, at sixteen, already pregnant with his eldest brother. They are speaking intimately together, alone, for they are away from the rest of the family for a few days staying at a health resort. The boy, Laurent, has been diagnosed with a heart murmur and has been sent to take the waters at a spa. The detail is one to astonish viewers in Britain or the United States, where a more puritanical tradition defines what is accepted as appropriate in terms of medical knowledge and advice.

The film begins at the time before the boy's illness, when he is still well and keeping up his attendance at school. But as Malle invites us to see it, the education at the hands of priests which Laurent is receiving also exposes him to an intimacy that is unsought. Here, a priest who teaches him in one class is also free to interrupt other lessons and to send for Laurent to come to his room. His right to do so is unquestioned since he sends for Laurent on the grounds that as a priest he is going to hear his confession. But this priest always makes sure to send for Laurent during his games lesson, as the other boys have not failed to remark. This way, once Laurent has knelt down by him to tell his sins, the priest can reach over to stroke the thigh that is left exposed by Laurent's gym shorts.

As a viewer, I find myself uneasy at this sight, more uneasy I would guess than one who had not been brought up to look on priests with respect. It's not clear to me that my unease is all on behalf of Laurent. I am uncomfortable in myself, it seems to me, at being asked to register information that is usually kept hidden. It is the invitation to see desire in a priest from which I hold back. Yet the evidence offered by such an example is important. Going back to what we know about the child and to the human blueprint, where the need for tenderness is matched by the need to find out, we may ask: what happens to these needs in an adult? For adults freedom and independence of thought and action are the objects of desire as much as intimacy itself. What is the effect on the inner life, we may ask ourselves, what happens when these objects are forbidden, as all of them are in the case of priests? Under Catholicism, these are men who have committed themselves to celibacy and, like soldiers, to obedience.

Malle makes us see the wish for intimacy in the priest, a wish whose complexities are crystallized in the image of his caress of the kneeling boy. Seeing it, we know that his desire has been made furtive and even twisted when it was turned away from women, becoming linked instead with humiliation. Uneasy as a viewer may be, Laurent himself is matter-of-fact in the situation, maybe never having had any illusions about priests to shatter. 'Can I go now?', he asks, knowing that the purpose of the meeting has been accomplished. For him there seems to be no question of shock or trauma; for one thing, it is no secret from the other boys. The viewer, however, may find it difficult to forget the sad, dissociated longing of the middle-aged man. As a Catholic priest he is expressly forbidden all intimate human contact, but he can't stop himself from reaching out in longing to touch the flesh of the young boy.

Malle frames this story with a wider world, the world of colonial relations and of war. In doing so he makes room for himself to remind viewers of the soldiers who have been taken to epitomize manhood and of the dangers that this identification brings. The year is 1954; it is the moment of the battle of Dien Bien Phu, in which the Vietnamese were fighting for their independence from France, which had been ruling Vietnam as a French colony under its own name for it of Indochine. With great care the movie is set in Dijon, an ancient city of southern France, which was itself under German Occupation less than ten years before. A number of conversations in the film draw attention to this timing and to the implicit context of resistance to a colonizing power. In the opening shots, Laurent is out collecting with a tin on behalf of the *mutilés de la guerre*, the French soldiers who have been disabled in the war, arguing passionately on their behalf in the face of indifference from adults. Not all his classmates are as sensitive to the realities of war and to what it costs: the figure of another boy makes us appreciate this, one who not only dresses like a tailor's dummy, but has not a thought in his head. Parroting a facile nationalism, he already sounds like an old man. As for Laurent, he reads a good deal and he thinks for himself. He appears to be drawing his own life from an inner world, where it is possible to keep his distance both from the emotional disturbance that is associated with the man of God and from the inner emptiness that comes with surrendering a mind of one's own.

His mother is conscious that her sons are leaving one world for another, cutting themselves off from her in feeling as they become men. We understand this ourselves, as audience, when we see her two older boys loose in her bedroom: they catch her up in a slightly menacing game, throwing her purse from one to the other, while she laughs but expostulates as they make off with her cash. 'You're already robbing me of too much', she protests. 'Do you think that you're a man?', she asks Laurent. His answer is 'No.' Instead he clings, this boy who is so eager to discuss questions of philosophy with his friends, to the intimacy and the emotional intelligence of his talks with his mother.

In this family, those who do consider themselves to be men know about women only in ways that are estranged, alienated in some way or codified. Laurent's father, who was once 'irresistible' in the beard that made her think of Garibaldi, the Italian freedom fighter, as his mother recalls, is now a consultant gynaecologist. 'What's that like?', her son asks her. 'You get used to it', replies his mother, meaning perhaps that she has got used to living with this substitute for an interest in what she herself as a woman thinks and feels. As viewers we connect this information with what we observe for ourselves, when we see that there is no longer any spark between husband and wife. In this world desire has moved out of marriage and away from relationship. Before he leaves for the spa with his mother, Laurent's brothers arrange a sexual initiation for him at the brothel where they are already regular clients, in spite of the marked reluctance he displays. An important part of the experience that they set up seems to be infusing heterosexual love with shame for their younger brother. The prostitute herself behaves gently and sensitively with the young boy to whom she has been assigned but his brothers, who are still under twenty themselves, get drunk and break into the room. By the wish of his brothers, Laurent's first experience of sexual intimacy with a woman, the act which is supposed to mark his transition into manhood, also charges that intimacy with shame and humiliation.

Some people might shrug their shoulders, saying 'Boys will be boys', but that response seems to beg the question. It is as though these young men were acting under a compulsion, just as I found myself doing when I turned away from my mother at thirteen. They too seem to be staging the repeat of an experience that they know without being able to give it a name: in their case too I would read that experience as the 'violent change' on leaving their mothers which first introduces shame and of which Suttie speaks.

But Laurent himself appears somehow to have avoided making that move out of his mother's world. Once arrived at the hotel in the spa, mother and son find that a secretary's mistake has meant that only one bedroom has been booked. Another bed is moved into the sitting room, bringing mother and son into a physical proximity that makes the intimacy between them even more intense. Laurent already knows that his mother has a lover, for he has seen her with him, just as the camera has revealed her to us also on the streets of their home town. 'What a thing for a boy to see', some old echo in me seems to exclaim. But though the discovery was significant to him, as he stood gazing from the window, accompanied by the old woman who brought his mother up, the movie does not present the moment as traumatic, or as an experience that Laurent cannot absorb. Rather it presents this moment as one when sight clears for him, when he recognizes his mother as a sexual being with a desire of her own and a life that goes beyond caring for her family. Once they are away together at the spa resort, however, there comes a crisis in her affair, when her lover presses her to leave with him for Paris. Though she refuses and returns to her room in the hotel, she is unable to hide her distress from her son.

Weeping as she explains, she repeats that for her love involves freedom; she had to part from him when her lover had wanted her to organize her life around his. 'The cheek of it!', cries Laurent, 'What about us?' For him, the shock is not that his mother should have a lover but that any lover should ask a woman to unmake the complexity of her own life in order to make him its centre. 'Never mind', he comforts his mother, 'one day you'll meet someone who loves you for the person you are.' Louis Malle may be anticipating a certain surprise in his audience, perhaps even some dismay at this picture of a boy who has no illusions about marriage. Could he be attempting to disarm these responses, to meet them halfway, when he makes Laurent's mother exclaim ruefully 'What a conversation between a mother and son'? But as Laurent reminds his mother, he is a son who also describes himself as her friend.

This scenario is set up in direct challenge to the ancient tradition of thinking which is symbolized for us in the story of Oedipus, the man who does not know his own mother when he meets her face to face, a story which represents closeness between mother and son only in catastrophic terms. Malle takes this challenge right to the edge, when the movie goes on to stage an act of incest between mother and son. Viewers are made to experience the full tension between repudiation and acceptance of what they see. 'What do I feel myself, does this act between these particular people and in these circumstances ask to be described as catastrophic?', he would like us to ask. Bastille Day arrives, the day that celebrates revolution and escape from the prison of the ancien regime, another date that has been carefully chosen to help us read the story. There are fireworks and dancing. Late in the evening, exhilarated and exhausted, somewhat tipsy too, laughing off admiring advances in the street, the mother returns with her son to the hotel where he helps her, rather in the way that a daughter would, to undress.

She has already established that she has none of the qualms about modesty that an audience might expect. If Laurent holds back from accepting the identity offered to men, it may be because his mother has refused the place that is conventionally offered to women. 'Don't look at me like that', she has said briskly, speaking to us viewers as much as to her sons as she moves round her bedroom in her underwear. 'I'm just not modest. Your father's never got used to it.' Laurent's mother refuses to collude with attitudes that would make her as a woman vulnerable to humiliation; 'Don't expect me to feel shame', she warns. She is not prepared to have her body viewed as a spectacle, in the fashion which cinema usually exploits; when Laurent spies on her in the hotel as she takes her bath she slaps his face. The conditions which regulate intimacy between them are already clearly established in the viewer's mind when, in half-darkness, we watch from the audience as the gentle touch of the hand that passes between mother and child, as they lie side by side, becomes transfused with the energy of an eroticism that is adult, and they become lovers.

'I don't want you ever to be sorry or ashamed about what happened', is the next thing that we hear. Instead of an authoritarian voice, speaking in condemnation or despair, a voice that each member of the audience has inside them, ready to give tongue, a mother's voice speaks into the silence. Most listeners probably feel it as the silence of shock: we have been made to look, as it were, directly into the sun. Catastrophic destruction is what we now expect. Yet moment by moment passes and the sky does not fall. When she tells her son that this act will never be repeated, that they will never discuss it and it will remain their secret, the mother appears to create a bridge over which they can move forward, leaving the dangerous and ambiguous moment behind.

It appears that according to the mother's reading of the matter a serious mistake has been made, one whose gravity she does not underestimate, for we later see her with eyes red from weeping. But she takes it as her immediate task as his mother to find a way of fending off shame from her young son. In the talk of secrecy, however, and her injunction to silence, for many viewers a red light will continue to flash. Secrets cut off those who share them from the rest of the community, and the burden of secrecy is very often part and parcel of abuse. Such a secret might be expected to come between Laurent and any future partner. As viewers we do not know what the future will hold for the relationship between mother and son or whether this act of incest will be repeated. Yet Malle frames their act of incest in a manner that is quite distinct from the way he presents the groping attentions of the priest, which are shown as a recurring event.

The kind of slippage from one form of tenderness to another that Malle shows here is one that is carefully situated in terms of time. It is restricted by the terms of his story to a moment at the age of fourteen. At that time the son was on the very cusp where the tenderness between parent and child, if it is to be carried forward into the emotional life of the adult, may start to be taken up into the mode of genital sexuality and passion. These psychoanalytic terms are not the ones that Laurent's mother would use, of course, for as she tells us herself in the course of an early conversation with her son, she never went to school. In her, Malle gives us the opportunity to imagine a woman with a mind which has escaped the teaching that is offered to girls, separating them from men. Lacking formal education, as Malle presents her, he also goes out of his way to indicate that she has kept strong hold of her connection with her father. That father died before Laurent was born but when she tells her son about him, that radical politician who loved to dance, a man who like Garibaldi pursued freedom on behalf of others as well as himself, it is clear that knowing her father and being close to him has enfranchised her. In the world of this daughter and her father, one which Malle makes real to us by his movie, there seems to be no place for trauma, or for catastrophic transgression, the crisis deserving absolute punishment and from which no recovery is possible.

Malle is aware that many of his audience will have difficulty in accepting this shift. He tackles the problem by choosing to play with them and to tease. Within a few shots Laurent is seen waking by the side of a girl of his own age, one who could be taken at first sight for his own mother, appearing to confirm such viewers in their worst fears. But the facts are less disturbing. The film-maker has Laurent move directly from his mother's room to the door of one girl after another, searching through the hotel, until he finds one who will take him into her bed. Tiptoeing back next morning into the rooms he has been sharing with his mother, he finds that his father and his brothers have arrived to join them.

His mother looks as though she has been crying, possibly in distress at what has passed between herself and Laurent, though it might also have something to do with the father's anger. As Laurent comes in, his father sternly asks where he has been. It is as though the law of the father and his rule have been reinstalled. But in the face of the father's demand for obedience, Laurent himself begins to laugh. In the closing shot every member of the family, one by one, including his mother, still only just over weeping, joins in. Some viewers will think that they are laughing at his embarrassed return: I would once have said myself that they were acknowledging something comic in desire. But now I would go further and guess that it is at the pretensions of the father, so futile in the face of the reality of his son, armed with a desire of his own, which makes him an independent creature, that Malle thinks we all ought to be laughing.

Watching *Murmur of the Heart*, I seem to be seeing eye to eye with Malle, sharing a vision of the struggle against separation that has to be fought by both sexes on the way to adulthood. The world that Malle shows me as a man is the one that I saw myself as a girl, but from a different point of view. In order to frame an act of incest for an audience and to do it responsibly, to present it as an object for the intelligence rather than for titillation, he has not isolated the act but presented it as part of a world view. In his movie desire, which includes the wish both for closeness and for independence, only becomes a predatory force when it is systematically and repeatedly thwarted, as in the figure of the celibate priest.

Providing resonance for my own scepticism about the use of incest as a bugbear, from which we are urged like children to turn away our eyes, Malle points instead to other forms of damage, ones that we have learned to overlook. As he invites us to see it, by tradition certain forms of mutilation are systematically induced in men. Reminding us of the cost of being separated from women in the name of ideal manhood, like the figure of the soldier and the priest, Malle prompts us to wonder about the readiness to accept that high price on men's behalf. Can we continue to overlook the deformations men are asked to undergo? Even Laurent's father and his brothers, whose choices about how to live have not been so austere, make a virtue of their emotional distance from his mother. She continues to see her job as a mother in terms of protecting the life that is in her son. In her refusal to accept the lesson of shame or to allow it to be passed on to Laurent, this woman without education takes her stand. It is one outside the tradition which idealizes manhood and in doing so passes on a disposition to abuse. Only by stepping outside this tradition, as the movie implies, going beyond the fear of punishment that has become associated with intimacy, can the lives of children and their emotional integrity be preserved.

Jennifer Montgomery:
Art for Teachers of Children

Malle's account of the dangers to a boy at adolescence offers confirmation of my own experience as a girl. The invitation to turn away from the parent of the opposite sex, in the name of being recognized as a woman or a man, poses dangers to the inner life and to adult identity that have not been widely named. Compounding the early separation that I have been describing comes a later demand to shut down the perception of desire in the opposite-sex parent, to stop seeing the longing for freedom in them alongside their longing for intimacy, a demand also to ignore their own drive to understand. It is not difficult to see how this might lead on to cruelty towards others and in the end also to cruelty towards the self. But because the impulse to know is built into the human blueprint, the impulse to reclaim this knowledge will return. I have experienced its power for myself in the drive to reconnect with my father. Understanding the part that is played in all of us by the impulse to reclaim a lost intimacy, often in the name of freedom, and at the same time to regain control of perception is our next task.

This dual impulse may take forms that appear to be innocuous, ones based on the search for knowledge. According to the movie, Laurent's father has chosen to study gynaecology, a profession which brings him into the most intimate contact with women. In the consulting room, however, as the doctor, it is he who occupies a position of authority as the source of knowledge. His women patients defer to him while submitting to his intimate touch. We know that many women have mixed feelings about this relationship and the position in which it places them. So too there are those, patients and therapists, who are unhappy about the power of the therapist in situations of an intimacy which is psychological, where patients allow themselves to open their hearts and trust to have them interpreted by one who is more knowledgeable than themselves. These professions have much in common in that they claim to be involved in making people better and in explaining an inner world that is hidden. They also recall the work of teachers and the vulnerability of their pupils, the vulnerability even of those who are no longer children.

At first sight the relation between teacher and pupil might seem much less intimate than those I have been describing. But in the classroom teachers also are offered access to a private inner world, when they are entrusted with training the mind. There the teachers' way of knowing, or at least the way of knowing that they represent, carries superior weight. When forms of knowledge which are abstract and intellectual are given precedence, other ways of knowing, ones that are more instinctive and grounded in the senses, like intuition, may be pushed to one side.

There is enough casual hostility to teachers as a group, enough attempts by government to regulate and re-regulate them, leaving them little freedom of action as professionals, both in the UK and in the US, to make us suspect that at a deep level an enduring hostility to that group is widespread. Such hostility may well coexist with tremendous gratitude towards individual teachers. It is in the world of education, I would argue, and in the name of furthering development and wholeness that the blind impulse to assert mastery of perception while ensuring mastery of close relationship is played out.

I see the world of education as offering an institutional form for such impulses, but it is also true that particular individual life histories and above all experiences of loss can lead to these impulses being precipitated compulsively in the form of sexual abuse. I shall say more about this when discussing Sappho Durrell's account of her father. I would like to begin, however, by asking some questions about sexual relationships entered into between students and their teachers, those who stand *in loco parentis*, in the place of a parent to them. I want to suggest that 'abuse' is not always the best way of describing these relationships.

At the age of fourteen, while she was still at school, the film-maker Jennifer Montgomery had an affair with one of her professors.

Stating this so baldly seems to close off most reactions except the one which has now become a kind of orthodoxy, which is to describe what happened in terms of victims and of sexual harassment, even of abuse. Most of us are familiar with campus romances for which those terms, or others such as 'exploitation', are not inappropriate, yet that still might not be the whole story. What about the Frenchwoman who exclaimed at a friend's dinner table 'But at university my friends and I competed to seduce our professors'?

At about the same time in the late twentieth century as the west began to recognize the problem of incest and child abuse, sex between teachers and pupils also become a public concern. This may represent a profound recognition, if one that was unconscious, for as Lévi-Strauss pointed out, sex between a girl and 'a man old enough to be her father' can be seen as an act of incest, reading metaphorically. The relationship between women students and their male teachers, or indeed between male students and the women who teach them, may be especially intense: even teachers who are not much older than their pupils are acknowledged to stand in the place of a parent. For both parties a dynamic moment from the beginning of life may be evoked, unbeknownst to themselves, a moment of closeness and of expansive discovery.

Nowadays every educational institution in North America and many in the UK publish statements condemning sexual relationships that cross the divide between teacher and student. Though at first sight it may seem a desirable one I would argue myself that this move is at least open to question. It is surely no bad thing if naive or unsophisticated students are put on their guard, yet the assumption that power lies only in the hands of the older person, who is nine times out of ten a man, seems to be seriously flawed. In these statements of university policy an old story is re-enshrined, the story that presents young women as having no desire of their own, as lacking most of all perhaps in the desire to know.

But the story that Montgomery tells in *Art for Teachers of Children*, the movie that she made when she was in her thirties, is a different one. She it was who took the initiative in the affair. 'There is a time when girls suddenly take charge of their lives and act on their desire', she told an interviewer. 'It's the way they discover their desire, by acting on it.' Though she believed that she had indeed been damaged by her relationship with the man in question, she was not left so traumatized by it that she was helpless. When the FBI made contact with her some years later, wanting her to testify against him, she refused. Like Laurent's mother, she distanced herself from the way of thinking which deals in separation and punishment. Instead, she set out to make a film about what had happened because she wanted, as she said, to understand.

Her uncertainty is reflected in the way that her movie presents its story obliquely and without any attempt to round out a full narrative, leaving us as the audience to complete the statement that it makes. That once might have seemed a baffling challenge, but readers will find that we are now equipped to match the images which she offers against the framework of understanding that we ourselves now bring. As an independent film-maker, Montgomery distances herself from Hollywood models of love and relationship, not least by a deliberate refusal of glamour in her heroine. In the movie, the young woman who plays Jennifer is not a vamp, deploying a battery of sexual signals to focus masculine attention. Instead, it is with an uncanny echo of Suttie and his talk of premature separation that she opens. 'I wasn't ready to be away from home', is the comment with which her voice-over begins.

As she presents it in this movie Jennifer's inner world appears to be one from which pleasure as well as confidence has leaked away, almost as though she were offering a direct image of the desolated world created in the young child. But this is a world not unique to the film-maker, for it appears to be shared by the young man who is her teacher and by his wife. It is in this emotional landscape that they all meet, perhaps one might say as survivors. Set in the bleak spaces of her dorm, the film shows the door of the apartment where her advisor lived with his wife as one that opens the way into a more peopled, less lonely way of living, perhaps one that reminds her of home and of a door that was once open there. Montgomery's advisor is no sophisticated seducer; to this viewer at least, the professor looks scarcely older than the girl who comes and parks herself in his office to talk about how she's feeling and to hear the clichés that he deals out to her in the name of encouragement and reassurance. 'I was his job', the Jennifer character explains. Under these limp, sullen words, did she feel that this teacher owed her something, owed her perhaps relationship with her father? It seems that like myself Jennifer had been robbed of this in the course of her education, in the sense that she has no way of representing her connection with her father for herself. Though her mother's voice is heard, there is neither sight nor sound of her father in the film.

She has been pressuring her advisor for some time before he gives way, if pressure is the word for a kind of stubborn repetition, one which sounds more like resistance and refusal than desire. Where Laurent's mother could speak directly, saying 'I want/I can't/I don't want', Jennifer, the educated daughter, falls back on a language that is impersonal and regulatory: 'It's time for her to lose her virginity and she'd like to lose it with him', becomes Jennifer's theme. In speaking of 'the time for her to lose her virginity' having arrived, Jennifer takes on the voice of a textbook in developmental psychology, or rather that voice displaces her own and speaks through her. This may explain why Montgomery chooses film as her medium, one where visual images, the language that existed before words, will be used as a test of them and asked in their stead to carry meaning.

Deaf to her strange use of language, the professor also shows that he is blind to her vulnerability as his student, when he takes up her offer, moved in turn by his own needs. These are ones that as audience we will have to deduce, for he is almost silent. One way you could frame this relationship is to say that the young woman in the film, having grown up in the Puritan tradition of New England, is at last impelled to wrest something in the form of words and deeds that acknowledge her body and its link with pleasure from her mentor. 'Fishing for compliments', he puts it grudgingly, not understanding any more than she what is driving her. When she wonders about pleasure and about her own place in the world, about the course that her life is going to take, and raises these questions with her mentor, we see that she is at odds with her education and with the view of herself as a woman that she has been offered there.

There is not much joy in the experience for either party: it seems that Jennifer's mentor, formed by the same Puritan culture as herself, is in no position teach her about pleasure any more than he is able to act with full responsibility towards her. Although he mimes concern, he too seems confused, an empty shell without ideas or responses of his own, like Malle's boy dandy. Her would-be advisor is equally unaware of what might give her pleasure or put her in danger. In the darkroom, where they retreat to have sex for the first time, she sits on a working surface to be penetrated. 'Did I hurt you?', he asks, to be told 'A little', as she reaches for a paper towel to wipe the blood, a towel that we will later watch her filing among other college papers. No pleasure, no intimacy, no knowledge, in this college world.

Both parties seem to be making use of each other. Like Jennifer herself, the professor also seems to be frustratedly seeking connection, unable to find what he wants in relationship with a living woman – we later learn that his marriage was in trouble too – but turning instead to making images of what he wants. Oblivious, it seems, of the deeper need that might underlie his activities, he thinks that he wants to be a photographer, and he takes the opportunity to make hundreds of shots of Jennifer's naked body. In taking these photographs he creates images or representations that will stand in wordlessly for the connection with a female body that he is blindly seeking. Where we may see Jennifer as in search of the connection with her father which appears to have been obliterated from her mind, these images made by her teacher appear like the traces of a mother, compulsively reproduced. When the affair was over Jennifer figured out what he owed her in modelling fees, as she tells the audience in voice-over, but she didn't pass the information on to her former lover, because she was afraid that 'He would try to pay it to her.' She was not interested in exacting that sort of justice, or in levelling the score.

In distinction from the world by which she is surrounded and in distinction from its representatives in the FBI, it is not 'justice' that Jennifer longs for but some means which the relationship has not brought her of finding a language that will value her and make sense of the impulse that moved her as a young woman. Neither the relationship with the professor nor her education has brought her this. Yet it is left to us as spectators to make this deduction. In the movie, Jennifer herself articulates no conclusions; she stands back from analysis. Instead, she asks about what has happened, about what was driving her, as I did myself, by assembling fragments, memory traces, among them visual images and broken exchanges of words.

As an artist, she suggests a wider framework too, one that includes her relationship with her mother. What her mother has to say is important, important to both Jennifer and ourselves, because it is not obvious, as it ceased to be obvious to me in my own life and as it ceases to be clear to many girls, whether her mother's voice was one to which she should give her trust. A leading feature is made of this voice, which is brought to the audience over the telephone. The mother is disembodied, as perhaps her daughter experiences her, this woman who has herself been shaped by her culture before being asked to carry its voice, as she does in reporting the demands of the FBI. Although her voice is heard, Jennifer's mother is never seen on screen, a device that undermines her credibility, prompting us to scan for a gap between her language and the experience that it claims to represent. As audience we ourselves are made to feel the distance and to share the suspicion that exists between this daughter and her mother, yet it is a suspicion that we ourselves may be free to go beyond.

In a conversation with her daughter after the affair is over, the mother reports that she has been hectored by the FBI, who are demanding to know Jennifer's whereabouts. If there is one form of behaviour that is unambiguously placed in the film, it is the threats uttered over the telephone by a second voice, one that is male and which speaks for the FBI. It is as a police presence, rather than a clerical one, that Jennifer's inner world feels the pressure of male authority. There is no doubt about the unpleasantness of this voice as it presses Jennifer for her co-operation: it calls out to be resisted, as do the lies told by the FBI agent in disguise who pursues her to the artists' colony where she has gone away to work. When she is seen laughing with the other women artists there, arms around each other's shoulders, we may catch a glimpse of the creative energy and warmth that she was seeking but failed to find in school.

'I can't believe that we didn't protect you from him', cries her mother, in an elliptical moment, blaming herself. As hearers we are caught in momentary confusion: her words ring both true and untrue. Like Jennifer herself we too may have difficulty in hearing the love that her mother is voicing, hidden under her self-blame. Instead we may be tempted to turn to critique, to pointing out that Jennifer was no victim, under attack, that she was the initiator in the affair. Yet she did stand in need of protection, just as she needed to be protected from the FBI: Jennifer felt that she was harmed by the relationship that she chose, which only confirmed her in deprivation and inertia. Further-more, as the only sign that Jennifer had a father of her own, that 'we' spoken by her mother is a crucial trace. The voice of her natural father is drowned out by the voice of authority speaking through the FBI, which seems to have replaced him in his daugh-ter's imagination, just as the voice of the church may do in other lives.

'There is nothing more dangerous than boring men making bad art', the voice of Jennifer's mother exclaims. We might retort that the huge absence of Jennifer's father does not seem a good idea either, any more than its concomitant, the fact that in this film her imagination can only present a man in the figure of a failed mentor or an intrusive police presence uttering threats and lies. In this her imagination demonstrates Jennifer's inner resist-ance to the attempts of formal education to shape the way she sees. Nevertheless, it could be that in putting her finger on bor-ing men and bad art Jennifer's mother does have a point. In the movie, Jennifer's mentor seems lacking in curiosity. Although he is an intellectual by profession, he is not a man who asks ques-tions. There is no 'why me?' in his response. And though he may appear to make a turn towards art, the photographs he takes are not made, like Montgomery's movie, in order to understand and to move forward. Instead his acts of image-making become stuck at the level of compulsion and repetition, as the product of drives that impel without being understood. Why otherwise would he take 'hundreds of photographs' of Jennifer's body, and go on, as the FBI involvement suggests, to have more affairs later with others of his women students?

The unacknowledged desire, the dangerous desire behind this bad art seems to be an impulse which will not be suppressed, the impulse to reconnection with the mother and through that with women. It puts such a man at risk himself in a world which is dedicated to passing on the way of thinking by which separation is enforced. Even in this movie, in the world of Montgomery's imagination, the women artists are barricaded together against the man from outside. Knowing how strong is the prohibition against crossing the line of gender, for this professor and for other men too, maybe the only way of feeling safe getting close to a woman is by simultaneously reasserting his identity as a man, in making sure that he occupies the position of authority over her mind as her teacher.

Sappho Durrell

'How much do you know about depression arising from incest as vs *mental* trauma? Oedipal' Sappho Durrell asked, in a document dated 24 July 1979. Like Jennifer Montgomery, she too was a woman who had been taught to think for herself and who wanted to understand her own experience. Unlike the film-maker though, she had not chosen the moment of her sexual initiation. Sappho herself was a writer and her chosen medium was language. But when she asked the psychoanalyst Patrick Casement to help her it was in a voice that was not entirely her own. Wanting to be taken seriously by the man who as therapist stood in the place of her teacher, like Jennifer, Sappho too began to speak like a book.

She did not live to write a book of her own. In 1991 the magazine *Granta* carried an edited selection from the papers, consisting of journals and letters packed into carrier bags that she left with a friend before killing herself. In those pages she indicted her father, Lawrence Durrell, and she asked that they should be published once he too was dead. The items finally selected for publication in *Granta* date mainly from 1979, the year in which Sappho became Casement's patient, and they include a number of letters from her father, one of which he apparently signed 'Lover'.

Unlike Montgomery, who felt that she had been damaged but was able to put together a work of imagination that would carry her story, Sappho was able only to assemble a collection of pages, written fragments held together by no inner structure. Instead of naming what her father had done and telling her own story for herself, in these edited papers at least, Sappho approaches her own experience indirectly, by means of a reference to literature, taking a leaf as it were out of the analyst's book. The narrative in which she sees her own life reflected is not one from the past but from her own lifetime: she recognizes her life in the pages of a novel by Nabokov, one that we ourselves will be looking at in part II:

> Couldn't read *Lolita* (couldn't bear to). Just asked people what it was about. Only managed to find strength to read it six months ago. I was (*literally*) freaked. Blank. Then *anger*. 'Don't ever do that to me again' – told Pa without words.

Even when she was writing for her own eyes, in her private journal, she appeared unable to speak freely. This loss of voice, of which Sappho herself complains, is a classic symptom of trauma, as we have seen. As such, despite the doubts of her father's biographers, it constitutes a form of evidence. If her story were based on false memory, as one of those biographers surmised, it seems unlikely that the voice in which Sappho told it would manifest such clear symptoms of damage. Although she appears to have wanted to draw her experience to public attention, it is not clear, however, that accusing her father was her main object. Much is left to the reader to infer, as though it were up to them to know, rather than up to Sappho herself.

Where does this collection of fragments, with its implicit invitation, leave us then as readers? Not, I suggest, in a position to play the part of detective or judge. Instead, we find ourselves poised to act as surveyors. Sappho's attempts to understand her own responses and to communicate with two men, one her father, the other her therapist, offer a field in which contours that are by now becoming familiar may be made out. I have chosen to situate Sappho's account by presenting it at this point in my argument, where a context for the relationships she is describing has been built up. At the same time I take her work as a cue to start drawing on the clinical experience of professionals in order to make comparisons.

Sappho claimed that her father had overridden her own wishes and forced her into sexual intimacy with him, throwing her inner life into a suspension from which she could not retrieve it to function again as herself. Her writing shows that something vital in her, the confidence that she understood her experience and could tell her own story, had been maimed. These might be the very powers that make a person human. Losing confidence in their ability to know appears to be common in survivors of incestuous abuse. When I asked Peter Lomas, the British psychoanalyst and writer, what he could tell me about people who had experienced abuse that involved incest, he replied 'They seem to have great difficulty in knowing whether it happened or not.'

I would argue that the original uncertainty which is installed in a child, when in the name of education they find themselves disconnected from their senses, becomes compounded when abuse takes a sexual form. At that point, too, the confusion between pain and pleasure in which I myself was taught to live as a girl takes on a new dimension. As Lana Epstein, a Boston trauma therapist, explained:

> Young people are sometimes told that they are enjoying the abuse: because they are usually inexperienced, they may be further confused by the reflexive response to sexual stimulus in their own body. This may lead them to doubt their own unwillingness to be abused: do they really want what is happening in spite of themselves?

Doubting the reality of their own wishes, the ground is taken from under their feet.

When Lawrence Durrell chose to name his second daughter Sappho for the lesbian poet who killed herself, it seemed to her that her father had pre-empted her life and her sexuality from the start. Sappho took the power of stories very seriously, more seriously perhaps than most people do. As a writer herself and the daughter of a writer, she knew that stories organize the imagination and pass on a vision of the world. 'I need to sort out reality from myth', she wrote. In making this attempt she found herself struggling not only against the language of therapy but also directly against her own father and against his voice in the present, when he insisted on defining the every day world for her: 'he will not give in over a single detail of reality', she wrote.

This is not the Durrell who is known to the world as a writer, one whose imagination dwells in a life that is remote in time and distanced by fantasy and romance. It is the father who had come to his daughter's room, when she was staying with him in the south of France, aged fifteen or so, soon after the death of his second wife, according to the oblique and angry references that are left for readers to piece together in the *Granta* papers. It is difficult to be sure whether the episode to which these notes refer was a single one that lay nearly twenty years in the past at the time when Sappho took Casement as her doctor, or whether she is describing an experience that was repeated, so sparse are the details offered in the published papers. Either way, it continued to stand between father and daughter and to shape their relationship – to shape her relationship too with the man she turned to as her doctor.

When Sappho put her question to Patrick Casement, she was showing him that as an educated woman she participated in his intellectual world and could speak its language. She made it clear that she wanted to be treated with respect and that she was ready to put forward alternatives of her own in order to name what she was feeling. At the end of the seventies when Sappho was writing, trauma was still a specialist term and had not yet passed into common use. 'What about thinking in terms of depression, as distinct from trauma?', she asks, trying out alternative ways of naming her own distress, maybe looking for one that sounded less technical and would fit more closely with feelings in which sadness and shame combined with a buried rage.

How difficult it would prove for her to make her voice heard is revealed in the pages of her own writing that *Granta* published, pages in which she can be seen struggling to find language, to name her experience for herself and to speak in her own voice. It was a struggle which was not helped by the language of therapy or by its dynamic, where the therapist, not the patient, is usually cast as the one who knows. 'Casement: . . . you don't want to hear certain things about my father or to consider them deeply because they strike a chord in you of something that you should have resolved and come to terms with and so you are trying to shield him', she wrote in accusation.

As a therapist, Casement was offering to interpret Sappho to herself. In traditional psychotherapy both language and dynamic revolve around the name of Oedipus and return inevitably to his story, one that concerns knowing and not knowing. In that world Oedipus the father is king and the place of a daughter is to accompany her father, her blind father into exile. But Sappho was already involved in resisting exile: that is she was resisting exile from her own self. She complained that her part in the human story had been assigned before she was born. In this she was doing something more than registering pique: bearing in mind what we have seen of the paths that are laid down for a daughter to follow, ones that take her away from her father and her brothers, we may feel that Sappho was putting her finger on something real.

The struggle for meaning in which Sappho and her father were caught seemed to be echoed when she found herself face to face with her analyst. She was unable or unwilling to speak freely in Casement's presence, though I would hesitate to read this exclusively as a symptom of sexual abuse. In conditions of intimacy with one who has authority, for any woman, particularly for any educated woman, the difficulty of trusting that her perceptions will be honoured is real. 'The problem is centred around expression. It's all tied up, so much so that I need constant prompting by an analyst. My mind doesn't want to let anything out, but I do. It's programmed to cut at certain intervals.' Divided against herself, Sappho both wanted to speak and refused to do so within a framework of relationship where she was the object of interpretation, not the interpreter.

Writing in her journal, however, her voice cleared. 'I need someone who can help me find my strength to dissolve what he's set up in me and to dissolve it in him without destroying him', she concluded. In this astonishing intuitive insight, one that was arrived at in isolation, Sappho Durrell diagnosed both her father and herself. She suggested that the source of his abuse was an artificial structure of feeling, a deformation of the inner life, one which she identified with her father but also recognized as one that had been replicated and passed on to herself. In spite of the rage she felt against her father, she grasped that something impersonal, a rigid inner model, as it were, had been involved. Prevented from knowing her own power of mind as she had been, she still guessed that in the minds of women like herself and their supporters might be found a key.

In the year she started her therapy with Casement, an article was published that broke the silence around experiences like her own, when Judith Herman and her collaborator Lisa Hivschman's piece on father–daughter incest came out in *Sciences*, the journal of the New York Academy of Science. Herman wrote of the prevalence of abusive incest and of abuse by men holding exclusive authority within closed communities. The article confirmed Sappho's experience and in this way offered her some support. It suggested that recognizing abuse as an everyday occurrence meant asking questions about the community as a whole and about the risks of distinguishing fathers by granting authority to them alone. Sappho wrote to Herman asking for advice on further reading and for the names of others working in the same field. She planned to write an article for the magazine *Spare Rib*. She drew up a bibliography for herself. She brought to bear all the resources of a highly intelligent woman who was also highly educated.

It is striking how close she was both in her self-awareness and in her difficulty with speaking not only to Jennifer Montgomery but also to the first women patients who came to Freud, the ones who told him of the experience of sexual abuse which he later dismissed as fantasy. When a younger man, Sandòr Ferenczi, would set out to speak about sexual abuse, he too would find himself fighting not to be silenced. Half a century later, in spite of all her courage and intelligence, Sappho did not feel that she had been able to command a hearing and in the end she gave up on the attempt to speak for herself. When she chose to kill herself by hanging in 1984 it was by an act that cut off her voice.

The work of therapists, however, gives resonance to one of her simplest observations. According to Sappho it was when she was around the age of fifteen that her father made his sexual assault. It was in May 1966 that she turned fifteen. Some seven months later, on 1 January 1967, Claude, her father's third wife, died rather suddenly. Therapists have observed that a state of mourning in the aftermath of a death, especially a mourning that is not fully voiced, can give rise to behaviour that is compulsive, to actions which are not rational or planned but produced without any intervening thought, rather like a reflex that is purely physical. When the actions cause no harm to others this is a relatively minor difficulty, but when the compulsion is to acts of sexual abuse, questions about motivation become urgent. There need be no mystery, however, about mourning and why it should sometimes be the trigger for acts of sexual abuse, if we look at the pattern of development which is imposed on children. I have been arguing that their inner life is shaped by a demand for separation, which gives rise to suppressed mourning, a mourning that is reintensified at the time of adolescence. Traces of this subterranean mourning can probably be seen in the lives of most men; Suttie connected it, for instance, with heavy drinking.

For certain individuals, however, depending on their life histories and on their circumstances, it seems that subsequent experience of loss, such as the death of a spouse, a parent or a child, can trigger the memory of that intense early mourning in a way that has explosive effects. Continuing to remain unspoken, the story of original loss still untold, mourning may now express itself in compulsive acts which take the form of sexual abuse. These could also be described as performances in which the original intimacy still living on in memory is staged. It is true that in these acts of sexual abuse the terms on which intimacy is reclaimed are not those of a child but the terms of an adult. Yet those abusing do not experience themselves as adults in this situation: psychologic-ally speaking they are operating out of a part of themselves that is much younger, younger, that is, in terms of years but at the same time older in terms of duration and of survival. Meanwhile, in the one they are abusing they seem only to glimpse a mirror of themselves.

Though abuse on the part of women is known to take place, by far the majority of reported cases of abuse are the work of men. For a man regaining conscious control after such an experi-ence the first imperative may be to reinstate distance, in order to reclaim his identity as a mature male and with it his authority. Once the tide of feeling has receded the false separations that seemed briefly to have been swept away have to be reinstalled. The choice would not be a conscious one but an instinctive adjustment on the part of the psyche in stabilizing itself. When Sappho describes her father's attitude towards her as a woman of thirty, she presents a man who is so intent on asserting his own authority as the one who knows that he is blind to other consid-erations. Lawrence Durrell did not content himself with insisting that his own description of the world had to prevail over hers; he also insisted on enlightening Sappho about herself, speaking on one occasion at least of her 'rat-like super-ego'.

People are often surprised by the love for their parents in children which survives abuse. Sappho loved her father; the writ-ings she left bear witness to her struggle to remain in relationship with him. But words failed her when she tried to imagine con-fronting him with what he had done, as they did when she tried to feel natural in addressing him. When she wrote to him she used to make drafts and would go back later to annotate them for her own benefit, commenting on what she'd written, as if seeking a different, more authentic voice, or at least one that might carry conviction. She may have been trying to find a voice that her father would hear with respect.

Sappho understood what was going on between them, including the sexual intimacy which she claimed that he had forced on her at fifteen, as a struggle for power, one that was taking place at the level of language and interpretation. Many therapists agree in defining fathers who initiate incest with their daughters in terms of the desire for power. Yet we ourselves might want to pause. To speak of power is not to get to the end of the matter, as if differences in power were the bedrock of human lives. As readers we know that such differences have to be created and maintained by acts of enforced separation: to pretend otherwise would be to play straight into a fiction that was exposed two hundred years ago by James Cook. Instead of talking about abuse in terms of power maybe we should be asking also about impulses of resistance, a resistance that takes different forms in fathers and daughters. In the father the urge to undo a separation that makes no sense may be so blind that it leads to violence. But what if the form it takes in daughters were a fierce intellectual determination to understand?

Father Porter
and Cardinal Law

The philosopher Paul Shepard once remarked that in America you can see the implications of European culture being played out. I would put it a little differently myself and say that in the United States you can see what happens when the founding story, the myth about fathers being different which comes down to us from the past, is really believed and acted on. Those consequences came to light, in 1992, with the case against Father James Porter, a man who bore the name of father as an official title, when he was charged with multiple acts of sexual abuse.

Even for those not raised as Catholics this story is one of significance: though it concerns the behaviour of priests, we should not forget that in the *Dictionary* definition of taboo it was priests who were grouped with great chiefs, or in modern parlance with politicians, as those whose place is at the top of the heap. The part played by compulsive behaviour, by language that does not follow the curve of experience and by downright lies in a society which is based on separation and hierarchy, played as inevitably in the public realm of politics and finance as in the private, can be glimpsed through the window offered by this story of a corrupt church.

For the United States, 1992, the year after Sappho Durrell's papers were published, marked the moment when it became impossible to ignore the sexual abuse of children or to overlook the fact that its targets could be male. This posed a massive challenge to most versions of masculinity, the notion of what it is to be a man, for vulnerability is not usually a feature. When the fictions around masculinity became an issue at the same moment as abuse the key co-ordinates in producing abuse were exposed.

The Father Porter case, as it became known when the story was widely reported in American newspapers and on television, was not a story about a daughter who had killed herself but one that took its force from the official status of the man who was the abuser. Thanks to the initiative of Frank Fitzpatrick, who had himself been one of those abused and who now came forward, in 1992 some sixty-eight women and men joined together to accuse the man who had once been set over them as their priest.

Thirty years earlier, they alleged, in the 1960s, when they were boys and girls living in Massachusetts, a Roman Catholic priest, Father James R. Porter, used them for his own sexual pleasure. During his seven years as parish priest it was claimed that he abused dozens of youths, most of them altar boys. Because a case was being brought to court, the offences were named, using a language which did not disguise the violence mixed in with this sexual drive: molestation, masturbation, sex games and acts of rape were specified. It was also acknowledged that measurable damage had been done by this violence. A precise figure was put on it when the church agreed to pay a sum of $5 million in settlement before the case reached court in December 1992.

The story of Father James the priest has a fit that is complementary with the story of Sappho and of other daughters. Reading the father's story alongside those of the daughters, it appears that it is in a whole landscape of social connections, family relationships as they are planted out symbolically in the world, that sexual abuse takes place. It is anything but a private matter or a matter of idiosyncrasy on the part of individuals. As priest, James Porter stood in the place of the ideal or symbolic father and his parishioners were invited to acknowledge him by that name. Yet that idealization in connecting him with the sacred also set him apart from other men and isolated him as a celibate from all women. Louis Malle's film, where the priest reached out to fondle Laurent, took it for granted that the human system would not tolerate such estrangement from itself. It may have been a confused resistance in James Porter to that estrangement and that idealization which was driving him in his abusive acts.

Like Sappho Durrell, James Porter had turned to writing but the language with which his training as a priest had equipped him seemed designed to get in his way. It did not permit him to name or to describe his experience. The *Boston Globe* published an account of the petition which he had written in 1973 at the time when he successfully applied to the Vatican for permission to leave the priesthood. Reading it, one might well deduce that by 1973 what James Porter wanted was out, out of a position in which he found himself experiencing a compulsion to abuse children. That position and its link with abuse was what he dwelt on in his formal application.

No one has a more careful education in matters of ethics and morals than a priest. In theory, a man with this education behind him should be able to bring some clarity to the discussion of human behaviour. But there is a disturbing fogginess in his language when James Porter speaks of what he has done. The most explicit phrase he used, according to the report in the *Globe*, was 'it had become known that he was homosexually involved with a group of youths in the parish'. Apart from this, he spoke only of 'a problem', or of 'temptation' or of 'falling', as if he had no means of analysis at his disposal but only the language of guilt and blame. He said nothing of his own feelings or of the feelings of the children whom he had abused. If he did have words of his own for these, if his own voice was not entirely suppressed, it seems that he did not believe that discussing the emotional impact of the experience and its psychological meaning would be a priority for his readers in the Vatican. In addressing the Holy Father, as the pope is known, James seems to have believed, apparently accurately, that repudiating his own impulses rather than describing them, in effect choosing blindness, was what was required.

Yet James Porter had not failed to register that his compulsion to abuse was linked to the special distinction conferred on him by the priesthood. One reason that he asks to be allowed to stop being a priest is that after living for two years as a layman he finds that he can keep his urges relatively in check, so long as he does not function as a priest. It had been hard for him even to contemplate giving up that place of exceptional distinction: the *Globe* reported that two psychiatrists had recommended him to leave the priesthood, telling him that the priesthood itself was his problem, before he resigned himself to living as an ordinary man. The connection seems to be clear: at one point, when Porter had been relieved of his duties as a priest, a friendly bishop gave him permission to say Mass during the week. It was with this return to celebrating Mass that the acts of abuse performed on adolescents began all over again.

In the Mass, as in some other matters of Catholic doctrine, an injunction against bodily clear-sightedness is reinforced. When a priest utters a certain form of words over the bread and wine, Catholics are under the obligation to believe that these are transformed into the body and blood of the historical Jesus. Such rituals are often compared with theatre, but in this case we can see an important distinction between the two. Where theatre prompts viewers to compare what is seen with what is heard and to explore any gap between the two, in the Mass viewers, in the form of the congregation, are positively required to over-ride what they can see and to accept an interpretation that goes counter to the evidence of their own senses. This imposition of beliefs for which the foundation is not apparent is central to creating the fear through which the church rules.

When James Porter went back to taking the leading part in this ritual, he also went back to committing acts of abuse, acts that as his victims remembered might take place at the altar and in the chancel of the church or the sacristy, which adjoins it, not just in the nearby basement of the church hall. He felt compelled to stage them, as it were, in the most sacred spaces of the church. It seems that James Porter had a divided mind. While he longed to play the part of a priest, the only man who was allowed to say Mass, there survived in him, though in a highly dissociated form, something that looks more like resistance and refusal, the twisted remnant of sense.

In the presence of strong feeling for which we have no words, as every sitcom viewer knows, you get what we call 'acting out'. Porter deliberately engaged in desecrating the very sanctuary and the altar at which he said Mass, the privilege which set him apart from others, as though he felt compelled to attack the way of thinking that made himself special and the church sacred. Appropriating these spaces, he used them to stage a series of abusive acts in which the desire for connection and the wish to dominate, the distorted version of the old wish for love, were violently expressed, though mixed together and confused.

It is possible, too, that James Porter was telling his own story in the only way that was available to him. Contrary to common belief, children who have been abused do not necessarily go on to become abusers, but every abuser, as therapists explain, was once abused themselves. Maybe, as a concerned though distant audience, we should be asking what happened to James Porter in church at the time of his own adolescence.

The word 'hierarchy' comes down to us from ancient Greece, where it originally meant the rule of priests. What it means to be ruled by priests, by a caste or class rather than by elected officials, is spelled out in this case, not least by the behaviour of Cardinal Law. When news of this case first broke in 1992, the initial re-action of Cardinal Law, the Roman Catholic archbishop of Boston, was to lie. He dismissed James Porter as a one-off, an aberration that did not warrant public attention, even though the cardinal was privy to the confidential report made to the nation's Catholic bishops in 1985. This report had warned them that their institu-tions were facing law-suits involving similar cases and in associ-ated areas, suits seeking $1 billion in damages. He was aware of further information that was relevant, the fact that since 1985 churches of various Christian denominations in America had already paid out $4 million in response to similar claims. Cardinal Law appears to have had no compunction about lying or about putting other children who would come in contact with Porter at risk. What mattered more to him than the welfare of children, more to him than clear vision, one can only conclude, was rebutting criti-cism of the system which supported his own identity as a great chief.

In his own mind, James Porter had got as far as connecting his position as priest not only with the impulse to abuse but also with the apparent licence to do it in freedom, unobserved. No one, as it were, saw him do it. 'Why didn't the nuns notice that we kept our rear ends to the wall when he was around?', Judy White asked, as one of the women that he had abused when she was a girl. Though his behaviour had attracted attention while he was still working as a priest, in the 1960s, other priests in author-ity over him did nothing. 'Why did no senior priest or cleric blow the whistle and make it impossible for him to continue as a priest? Was there no adult ready to stand up?', a man identified only as Michael wanted to know. This oblivion, this inertia and silence may be traced directly to the church's own teaching, which actively fosters blindness through the ritual of the Mass. Catholics were taught to live in a parallel universe: 'We grew up thinking priests were the next thing to God', another of Father Porter's victims explained.

There were more human reasons for children to be attracted to him: James Porter was said to have been a big, handsome, outgoing man 'He was like the Pied Piper', one man remembered, comparing Porter with the fairy-tale figure who drew children irresistibly after him by his music, children who left their own parents to follow him. As a priest, James may have seemed to offer the promise of a perfect father, one who was never angry, just as he may have seemed to be the next thing to God. In a sense these children from Massachusetts never did return to their own parents: many of them spoke of the burden of guilt that cut them off from their families at the time when they were growing up. These parents, like the ones in the old fairy-tale, had their children stolen.

In spite of the deafness and blindness shown by the church as an institution, the old ways did not altogether prevail in this case. A turning point came in negotiations between lawyers for the victims and those representing the church when the new bishop, Bishop O'Malley, once he had been put in charge of the case, invited some of the men, though not apparently any of the women, to meet him and to tell him their stories. After that afternoon when a man in authority began to listen the dynamic was changed and negotiations went forward.

Looking back on their lives, survivors could put a name on the price that they had paid as children and on the impairment that had compromised their later lives. They could trace the effect on their careers and on their marriages. Not surprisingly, in many of these men, who had been betrayed by a man who had looked like an ideal father, the inability to trust and anger against authority went hand in hand. Male psychologists who interviewed them agreed that these men, by then around forty years of age, had continued to be affected by this adolescent experience throughout their lives. 'It was quite striking how dramatically the lives of these people had been affected', reported Dr Stuart Grassian. The notion of abuse as a transient emotional contretemps was seriously challenged, once it could be measured against job security and success in a man's world, criteria that made sense to other men. When the victims were men, there was clarity in the public realm, all of a sudden, about what happens when a younger person is forced or seduced into responding to the sexual needs of an adult. Terms such as 'serious psychological trauma' were freely used.

This marked a difference from what had been the usual experience of identified incest victims, who were preponderantly
women, at that time. It meant that the old hesitation on the part
of the public, the scepticism – did it happen, did it not happen,
is she just a hysteric – the same hesitation that would paralyse
Lawrence Durrell's biographers, could for the moment at least
be set aside. It took men to speak of their experience of abuse
before a public acknowledgement of its realities could be established. At the same time the snobbish delusion that abuse was
a problem of the uneducated and the poor was scotched. In
Grassian's words: 'For the most part they had all come from
stable and functionally secure homes. They were apple pie and
ice-cream kids who had gotten swept up in the compulsions of a
priest.'

A huge step in terms of demystification was made at this time.
Nevertheless, in spite of all the new clarity that was achieved,
one fiction seemed to remain intact, one underlying assumption
stayed unexamined and was enshrined in language. 'We're all of
us heroes, and every person who comes forward and faces vic-
timization is a hero', proclaimed Frank Fitzpatrick, the man who
first laid allegations in this case. The only language that was
available to these men, to offset the past humiliations which they
now braced themselves to admit in public, was the language of
heroism. It continued to go unrecognized, the danger of isolating
and idealizing individual men, calling them heroes like Oedipus or
comparing them, like Father Porter and his fellow-priests, with
gods. Masculinity itself, as a construct, with its fiction of purity
and separateness, survived all the negative publicity unchallenged.

Sandòr Ferenczi and Sigmund Freud

In the United States, recognizing sexual abuse as a reality stopped short of unmasking manhood as a fiction. Yet in Europe, even before the Second World War, the two had already begun to be linked in the mind of one man at least. The Hungarian analyst Sandòr Ferenczi worked with those who had been subjected to sexual abuse: when this brought him into conflict with his mentor, Sigmund Freud, he was led to asking about masculinity and the part masculinity had played in structuring his own inner life. In Ferenczi's personal experience the topic of sexual abuse and the problem of masculine identity were associated, even though he did not live to reflect on this fact in his writing as an analyst. It is by reading his published work alongside his private diary that we ourselves are put in a position to recognize the conjunction.

With the turn to Ferenczi the first part of this book moves into its last phase. The argument so far has been working to build an understanding of how abuse is constituted and to explore the experience of those involved in abuse, an exploration which culminated in the examples of Sappho Durrell and Father James Porter. We are going to find that the framework that has been established here by means of comparative readings and juxtaposed experiences is confirmed by independent evidence, the observations of analysts working with abuse. They too note the evidence of an intellectual abuse which is systemic, a silencing which pre-dates the moment of sexual abuse and compounds the difficulty in speaking of those who have been abused.

Most analysts would accept that their task is to assist the process of healing: those whose work I discuss here have found that to do this it has been necessary for them to give up the position of intellectual authority as analyst accorded to them by convention and to find a different relationship with those who come to them for help. They have found that setting up a community on different terms from the ones we are used to, the terms that rely on using categories to separate one group from another and on compliance, seems to be a crucial move in restoring those who come to them for help, however tiny that new community may be, even if it extends only to the couple of analyst and client.

With the story of Sandòr Ferenczi, which will be followed by an account of the work of analysts Valerie Sinason and Estela Welldon, we move on to listen to the voices of doctors writing about the clients who come to them following an experience of sexual abuse. In listening to their clients and in responding to them, all three have found themselves placed at odds with the intellectual and therapeutic traditions in which they had been educated and trained. In the case of Sandòr Ferenczi, with which we begin, it was the authority accorded to a father-figure that he found himself obliged to challenge, both in his theoretical writing and in his own relationship with Freud.

Sandòr Ferenczi lived in Budapest before the Second World War. He had trained as a doctor in Vienna during the 1890s and had gone on afterwards to train as one of the early psychoanalysts who worked with Freud. In this sense, he was a founder member of the twentieth century's new priesthood, whose members offered a new access to the unseen world. In Budapest he became known as the analyst of last resort, a man who would take on even those cases from which his more timorous colleagues shrank. Transvestites and other people whose sexuality took forms that were unacceptable came to him.

In September 1932, the Twelfth International Psychoanalytical Congress was due to meet in Wiesbaden, Germany. At that time Freud, whose seventy-fifth birthday was the occasion of the meeting, was already suffering from the cancer that would kill him in 1939, and he did not plan to attend. So Ferenczi visited him, a fortnight before the congress, in order to read him the paper that Ferenczi was intending to give there. He had originally planned to speak on 'The Passions of Adults and their Influence on the Sexual and Character Development of Children', but when it came down to writing the paper, Ferenczi realized that this topic offered all too much material for a single talk. Instead, he decided to narrow it down; the paper he read to Freud would be presented as 'The Confusion of Tongues between Adults and the Child: The Language of Tenderness and of Passion'.

That paper is now recognized as the classic discussion of incest. But it was many years before it could become widely known. Once he had heard Ferenczi and his argument out, Freud told him 'You can't give this paper.' Ferenczi declined to withdraw. When they parted, Freud refused to shake him by the hand. Nine months later Ferenczi, who had also been in poor health, was dead. Freud's move to ostracize Ferenczi and silence him would be repeated once his colleagues at large had heard what he had got to say. His paper was included in the conference proceedings and in another specialized journal that appeared in 1939, but it was not republished for seventeen years and was only translated into English by Michael Balint in 1955. It would be more than half a century before his ideas and insights would be more or less assimilated by the scientific community.

The head-on clash with Freud was only the culmination of a long struggle between the two. Freud was Ferenczi's analyst and he had very clear ideas about the path his friend should take. He wanted him to get more politically involved in the movement and to accept the presidency of the International Association. Freud dissociated himself from Ferenczi's drive to find a means of making his patients feel better: the pursuit of knowledge, he said, was more important to him personally than healing. He belittled Ferenczi's attempt to refine the ideas and techniques of analysis in the light of his special experience, writing them off as a rejection of Freud himself and referring to his impulse towards independence as evidence of 'a third puberty', calling him, in effect, a boy. This tactic still appeals to some therapists today: it can be tempting for them to pull rank, as we say, in order to dismiss information that might complicate their picture of the world.

Ferenczi and Freud had once been on terms of intimacy, when their ideas had agreed, and the older man's disappointment at this loss was joined with his wish to bring the younger one to heel. In a letter dated 12 May 1932 he wrote, as if to one who was refusing to take on the responsibilities proper to a real man, 'you must leave that island of dreams which you inhabit with your fantasy-children, and once again join in mankind's struggles.' After their abortive meeting he would write insultingly that he could not be bothered to point out 'the technical errors' in the conclusions presented in Ferenczi's paper because he knew that he would not listen. There is an echo of the playground – I know better than you but I'm just not going to share it with you – in the form that his angry grief takes.

There are no heroes in this painful story of two men impaled on the masculine identity that had supported their whole lives: Freud was seventy-five, Ferenczi fifty-nine years old. They had lived out their professional connection and their personal one within the pyramid model, where Freud as the founder of psychoanalysis stood at the apex as father. Rather like King Lear with Cordelia, now, Freud found himself and his paternal authority outraged. And Ferenczi himself discovered that there was no way forward for him; he no longer knew how to live his life as a 'man'.

On October 2 1932 he made a long entry in the clinical diary that he had been keeping since the beginning of the year:

> The insight this experience [with Freud] has helped me to attain is that I was brave (and productive) only as long as I (unconsciously) relied for support on another power, that is, I had never really become 'grown up'. Scientific achievements, marriage, battles with formidable colleagues – all this was possible only under the protection of the idea that *in all circumstances* I can count on the father-surrogate. Are the 'identification' with the higher power, the most *sudden* 'formation of the superego' the support that once preserved me from final disintegration? Is the only possibility for my continued existence the renunciation of the largest part of one's own self, in order to carry out the will of that higher power to the end (as though it were my own)?

For a number of years he had been working away on his own, with his own self-selected group of patients. That experience had given him a new distance both from the techniques in which he had been trained, his old way of working, and from the institutions which supported it. As he took the measure, now, of his clash with Freud, it allowed him to register the structure of his own personality, which was thrown into relief by the shock. As a man, he realized, his inner life had been organized in subjection to the image of a father, with whom he identified himself, and so felt safe. His sense of secure identity relied on that subjection. But now that unconscious edifice, which had been hidden from himself, lay in ruins, for Freud was withdrawing his support.

The many studies of masculinities made in the last decade follow on the widespread acceptance of the notion of gender; we have learned to see that it plays a key role in organizing the life of the community. It is widely recognised today that individual identity is structured along the lines of gender. It was many decades before that term came into use that Ferenczi recognized that he had been living his life as a 'man' and that this had somehow subverted who he really was. In spite of all the rhetoric familiar to us as it was to Ferenczi, the rhetoric that equates manhood with liberty, he noted in profound dismay that adopting masculine identity seemed to mean surrendering one's own freedom. Looking back, he felt that he had been living the life of a puppet or a slave, in thrall to the figure of an ideal father. What could he do? He knew that it was no academic question, that it was a matter of life and death. Ferenczi was a medical doctor and he made a link between the physical illness that had now begun to threaten his life, pernicious anaemia, and the crisis in his inner world:

> And now, just as I must build new red corpuscles, must I (if I can) create a new basis for my personality, if I have to abandon as false and untrustworthy the one I have had up to now? Is the choice here one between dying and 'rearranging myself' – and this at the age of fifty-nine? On the other hand, is it worth it always to live the life (will) of another person – is such a life not almost death? Do I lose too much if I risk this life? *Chi lo sa?*

Knowing, and the language in which to speak one's knowledge, were at the centre of the problem, as he recognized: who knows, Ferenczi wondered, *chi lo sa*? But, like Sappho, Ferenczi really did feel that he knew. Their experience of their own inner lives, and their reflections, had taught them both that the only way forward was 'rearranging' the self, or 'dissolving what had been set up' inside them, in Sappho's words. It was left to Ferenczi to name this internal edifice as the structure of male identity, or as we might call it today, the fiction of masculinity.

'I feel it in the marrow of my bones', we say when we know that we have no proof and could not argue a case but we still feel certain. Like Sappho, Ferenczi too died without finding a solution for the fiction of masculinity, which played such a large part in organizing and at the same time deforming inner lives. Sappho took her own life deliberately but Ferenczi was psychologically quite tough, so he speculated that for him illness would have to take a physical form – 'instead of falling ill psychically I can only destroy – or be destroyed – in my organic depths', he wrote in October 1932. He had often been teased as a hypochondriac on account of the anxious attention he paid to his body, but now Ferenczi was really sick and he connected this sickness with the crisis in his inner life. He registered what he knew deep in his body. Ferenczi's illness took the form of pernicious anaemia, a condition where the bone marrow no longer reproduces enough of the red corpuscles that carry oxygen round the body and keep it alive. He got sick when he registered that he had been harbouring what therapists today call a false self, one in which he himself could no longer believe.

In 'The Confusion of Tongues between Adults and the Child: The Language of Tenderness and of Passion' Ferenczi spoke of what he had observed to be misguided in the conventional attitude of therapists to their patients, making a link between this attitude and the behaviour that we call abuse. It is scarcely surprising that Freud was not best pleased when his younger colleague suggested that in their consulting rooms he and his colleagues were duplicating, in a sort of shadow form, the experiences that had first made their patients sick. It was an attack on the integrity of the person, a failure or a refusal to respect it, that had first done the damage, but the attitude of therapists was repeating the pattern, so he claimed. Ferenczi connected the therapeutic attitude in which he had himself been trained with the attitude of educators: he asked about the readiness of both to inflict distress on those in their care in the name of a higher good, punishing in the case of teachers, or insisting on keeping patients in a state of emotional deprivation as classical analytic theory did. Analysts were not supposed to comfort their patients but to observe them and use their distress to advance the analysis. Ferenczi suspected that the set of connections which he had unveiled pointed to a pathology that was in the culture and was culturally endorsed.

Ferenczi had begun to suspect that the forms of sexuality which we call perversions and which caused so much suffering were not the result of moral or psychological weakness but exhibited instead a quite specific response to external factors. It was the experience of sexual abuse which produced these 'perversions' as symptoms, among others which were also highly specific and recognizable. Observing his patients, Ferenczi came to be troubled, unlike many of us who might find it merely agreeable, by the sense of an undue compliance towards himself in them. It was after observing these patients closely and above all listening to them that he drew up his now classic account of the inner dynamics of abuse.

'It is difficult to imagine the behaviour and the emotions of children after such violence', he begins, inviting his readers to join him in stepping straight into confrontation with the taboo. Though you might imagine the child's response to be one of resistance, the actual dynamics of the encounter as he sets them out are very different. 'Instead of crying out "No, no, I do not want it, it is much too violent for me, it hurts, leave me alone"', the child is paralysed, as he puts it, by enormous anxiety. Instead of resisting the menacing person, a task for which the child is not psychologically equipped, being so much younger, it identifies itself with the adult.

This is no mere figure of speech. The child who is forced into sexual intimacy, according to Ferenczi, actually takes a print of the voice and language of the attacker. Its own wishes and perceptions are not only overwhelmed but they are usurped, when their place is taken by the desires and the views of the adult. This substitution is registered on the voice, for in shock the child can lose the power of speech and become dumb, while afterwards, its utterances pick up and parrot the voice and language of the aggressor. It becomes a sort of living record of the attack. Ferenczi's title, 'The Confusion of Tongues between Adults and the Child', gives that transfer focus:

> These children feel physically and morally helpless, their personalities are not sufficiently consolidated in order to be able to protest, even if only in thought, for the overpowering force and authority of the adult makes them dumb and can rob them of their senses. *The same anxiety, however, if it reaches a certain maximum, compels them to subordinate themselves like automata to the will of the aggressor, to divine each one of his desires and to gratify these; completely oblivious of themselves they identify themselves with the aggressor.* (original emphasis)

With these words, Ferenczi names the process by which children who are abused lose touch with their own bodies and the sense of who they really are. The damage that we have learned to recognize in terms of neurophysiology he represents in terms of the child's sense of identity. He names the process by which the integrity of the self can be shattered and the child driven out of its own body.

The body of an abused child is in a sense run, thereafter, by the abuser or their mental representation. Ferenczi was the first to recognize and name the process that we now know as introjection, the process by which a part of external reality is taken into the inner world without being grasped and digested as it were by the intelligence. He came to the conclusion that at the moment of abuse the child takes the figure of its aggressor intact and unmodified into itself, while ceasing to register the abusive act as a part of external reality. In the imagination of the child, the abuser becomes separated from their action.

The child has now only an imperfect memory of the event, one that is compromised. But from that time forward such children still have access to a refuge in the less confusing world that they knew before, because it lives on inside them at the level of fantasy. They do not give up what they once knew of a world where they were treated appropriately, or with tenderness, as Ferenczi names it, at the hands of adults.

'What was there to affront his colleagues in this?', we might ask ourselves. Why should his memory have been reviled and his work suppressed? But Ferenczi did not limit himself to offering a model of the inner world of the child, or suggest that the assaults he was describing were the work of a pathological few. That would probably have been discreet and avoided trouble. But instead, wanting to understand the genesis of abuse, he broadened his diagnosis and brought an end to the convention by which it was isolated from other social experience, marked off as an aberration from the values and behaviour of the healthy majority. On the contrary, Ferenczi observes that the impulse to abuse is often linked with religious zeal: 'not infrequently after such events, the seducer becomes over-moralistic or religious and endeavours to save the soul of the child by severity', he notes.

Ferenczi did not isolate the experience of sexual abuse, as if it were the only source of the trauma that he describes. Instead he noted that there are two other ways that children may be maimed, or in his own words 'helplessly bound to an adult', as they are following the experience of abuse. A child may be made into this virtual slave by exposing it to unbearable punishments, he observed. There is also the 'terrorism of suffering': where a parent's demand for care or evident need of it displace what are the true interests of the child. No wonder if Freud thought this too dangerous for public discussion. When he compared the sexual violation that is thrust on some children with other moments in which children are forced to adapt to the beliefs of adults and to their demands, demands that might otherwise have been seen as legitimate, Ferenczi linked sexual abuse with education and with a sickness that is passed down from one generation to the next.

In developing this most radical argument, it is on the threshold, where the child moves out from a care that is nurturing as distinct from one that requires the child to adapt to it and to change, that Ferenczi asks us to pause. 'Children cannot do without tenderness, especially that which comes from the mother', he observes, just as Bowlby would come to do. This is an observation that has been reconfirmed more recently by Colwyn Trevarthen when he noted how much reciprocity of attention between mother and infant is involved in early development. In this paper Ferenczi's extraordinary move is to set tenderness against adult passion and to compare them with tongues or languages that are foreign to each other. 'Why should this difference exist, what are its consequences?', he asks.

Experience had taught Ferenczi, a finding that has been confirmed by later therapists, that tenderness, or rather the lack of it, is often at issue when incestuous moves are made. You could almost say that a kind of mourning for the loss of tenderness, the loss of reciprocity, is involved. Children often believe that they are only playing, that they are in a game with an adult, a game in which the child itself is playing the part of an absent mother, when the adult shocks them by suddenly changing the rules. Substituting adult passion for a tenderness that the child was expecting and was all that they were equipped to handle is often the first move. It is this substitution of one touch for another that Ferenczi linked with a shift in language, the 'confusion of tongues' that takes place in the moment of abuse, leaving the child no longer able to find its voice or say what it wants in its own words.

Of all the consequences that he observes, loss of voice and language, loss of confidence in the perceptions, displacement from the body and loss of connection with the world, the one that Ferenczi singles out as the most important is the introjection, along with the rest of the adult persona, of the adult's feelings of guilt. 'The most important change, produced in the mind of the child by the anxiety-fear-ridden identification with the adult partner, is *the introjection of the guilt feelings of the adult*' (original emphasis). There is a point of particular interest here, where Ferenczi begins to make his boldest challenge to orthodox thinking and to press on the social origins of guilt. We might be tempted to imagine that the guilt of which he speaks is the adult's guilt at molesting a child, but that is not quite what he is asking his readers to recognize. Like other analysts, Ferenczi had been trained to think of guilt as normal, or as psychologists say adaptive, in adults and that adult sexuality, or passion as he calls it here, was inevitably tied up with guilt. For him, the guilt in the adult that the child was picking up at the moment of contact was not a guilt that was generated by the act of seduction but pre-dated it.

Like his more conventional colleagues, Sandòr Ferenczi had taken it as a premise that normal adult passion involved emotions that were ambivalent and contradictory, so that by definition the love-making of adults would be mixed with hatred and guilt. Taking that as a premise, he assumes that no further explanation is needed, when he refers to 'the hate-impregnated love of adult mating'. But as he brooded over the evidence he had found among his patients for a widespread set of mental structures that corresponded with the consequences of abuse, he was led to ask again about what constitutes normal development. If young children only develop and flourish under a regime of tenderness, a care that he describes as maternal, why should the language of adult intimacy be so different, so charged with hostility and with guilt? Could it be, he wondered, that the hatred and guilt which were demonstrably associated with mature passion – think of Othello – were not really integral features of human development as had been supposed?

Ferenczi knew that the proposition he was making, the suggestion that human behaviour as we know it cannot be taken as normal but is deformed in response to a traumatic intervention systematically imposed, was so radical that he himself could hardly take it in. It is so radical, in fact, that most of his readers seem to have avoided recognizing the wider political and organizational implications of his findings. So far as his work has now found acceptance, it is on the basis of his model of the after-effects of trauma on the inner life. The wider argument that he makes about the 'normal' treatment of children by 'morally responsible' adults as inherently damaging, and the links that he makes with taking pleasure in cruelty or in one's own suffering, are not taken up.

But Ferenczi, though he did not have the time left to him to develop these insights, knew very well that they were nothing less than revolutionary, that they would involve a recasting of the whole social system if they turned out to be true. Not only would 'certain chapters of the theory of sexuality and genitality', in Ferenczi's phrase, need to be revised. The question of the part played by what we have flattered ourselves is a civilizing process would have to be rethought: as Ferenczi put it, we would now have to ask 'How much of the sado-masochism in the sexuality of our time is due to civilization (i.e. originates only from introjected feelings of guilt) and how much develops autochthonously and spontaneously as a proper phase of organization'. Once we accept that a regular part of normal childhood experience, the experience of children who have not been abused but only excessively punished or been a witness to parental distress, once we accept that this experience seems to involve introjecting a guilt that is passed on by others and which is not understood, do we even know what normal development, development without this burden, would be?

Psychoanalysis had made a place for itself in the world at the price of identifying very strongly with the most respected intellectual traditions of post-Enlightenment rational thought, a way of thinking that is sometimes known as Cartesian, after the French philosopher Descartes, though like others it could fairly be described also as masculinist. Now, as Ferenczi points out, the identification of psychoanalysis with that tradition might be starting to look like a mistake. The Cartesian explanation of the human world, like the psychoanalytic one, revealed a blind spot. They took suffering, the experience of emotional pain, for granted as if it were a given:

> Psycho-analysis willingly agrees with the Cartesian idea that the passions are brought about by suffering, but perhaps will have

to find an answer to the question of what it is that introduces the element of suffering, and with it sado-masochism, into the playful gratifications at the level of tenderness.

Most of us can remember the pious tone in which we have been taught to expect pain and disappointment in this vale of tears. Going behind this assumption, however, Ferenczi suspected there lay a different explanation, one that was hidden. Philosophers and psychoanalysts alike were avoiding both history and politics when they held back from putting a crucial question. What if suffering and emotional pain were not inevitable responses to living but were gratuitous, that is they were a response to mutilation, the mutilation imposed on children in the name of improving them by education and fitting them to live as what we call civilized beings, as adult women and men?

There was no time for Ferenczi, who was already so ill, to pursue this question, but in the last lines of the postscript which he added to his original paper he appeared to be moving towards asking about the impact on human sexuality of those divisions by gender and race that were taken for granted. As he wrote, linking these concepts, 'The "Theory of Genitality" that tries to found the "struggle of the sexes" on phylogenesis will have to make clear this difference between the infantile-erotic gratifications and the hate-impregnated love of adult mating.' In speaking of 'the struggle of the sexes', repeating a phrase from a few lines earlier and so emphasizing it, Ferenczi was already gesturing towards the division by gender on which all civilizations that we know of build, and towards the familiar hostilities between women and men that this separation entails. We may also note his use of the scientific word 'phylogenesis', which means the history of a race or species. This was coined in 1866 at the very height of the attempt to prove whites were superior to blacks: at a subliminal level Ferenczi is beginning to point us as his readers away from myth and towards history, towards the politics which gave rise to the notion of race as a category.

Though he reached for the historically charged term 'phylogenesis', he was not able to take his intuitions further, or to explore the mechanisms which link the hostility created in the name of gender and the violence that is the consequence of division by race. That work was left for those like the African-American writer Toni Morrison and the novelist from South

India Arundhati Roy, whose studies of incest and abuse will be discussed in the second part of this book. Instead Ferenczi's own work ends with a question that had been elided by a whole intellectual tradition but which he himself refuses to give up: how does intimacy get contaminated by hatred and guilt in the 'normal' psyche?

Valerie Sinason and
Estela Welldon

To the question that was formulated by Sandòr Ferenczi, the voice of Ian Suttie, his contemporary and colleague, offers a response. Reading their work side by side, as the analyst Jane Suttie, who was married to Ian Suttie and also translated many of Ferenczi's essays, must have done, the separation that we have been taught to see between the world of abuse and the world of the 'civilized' and 'normal' disappears. That gap was produced by double vision, not clear sight. Brought back together into focus, these images of the world coincide. The territory of the 'civilized' and 'normal' where children are brought up by careful mothers, which is described by Suttie, and of which I myself have written earlier, is revealed as the everyday aspect of the world of abuse that is inhabited by Ferenczi's patients. Far from being worlds apart they share a common geography and feature similar emotional landscapes, while being governed, psychologically speaking, by an identical law.

'I need someone who can help me', Sappho Durrell wrote. 'I need to sort out reality from myth.' Like Jennifer Montgomery, she was out for clarity rather than vengeance. She wanted to save her father, if it could be done. 'I need someone who can help me find my strength to dissolve what he's set up in me and to dissolve it in him without destroying him.' Even for therapists, stepping outside the framework, the civilized blueprint that produces incest and abuse, is easier said than done. The example of Sandòr Ferenczi brings this home. Ferenczi believed that his own inner life, just like that of his patients, had been compromised and rendered false: he too felt that his independent identity had been shackled to the image of a father. Today there are many therapists who work with the aftermath of incest and abuse, yet it is not always clear that they have been able to free themselves from the old inner models and the patterns that they carry forward, patterns that are encapsulated in the story of Oedipus, the blind monster.

It is common among therapists to speak in terms of 'perpetrators' and 'victims', but this language seems to perpetuate a dangerous separation, reminding us of the original separation between women and men, which it seems only to reinforce. To think in those terms has become our default position, for even though we know that mothers too instigate abuse most people think of women as victims and of perpetrators as men. I have no interest in condoning the acts of those who abuse, yet handing out labels seems to shut down too many questions, as if once these were assigned there were no need for further insight or thought.

Yet insight is what those who commit acts of abuse also crave. Estela Welldon is a consultant psychotherapist at the Portman Clinic in London, which is run by the National Health Service, where she works with both abusers and abused. Most of the abusers treated there are not sent by the courts but refer themselves, often making contact by writing, she tells us. 'They want to understand why they are compelled to commit inexplicable acts.'

It is not consoling to admit this but there is a sense in which all therapists, like mothers, could be said to work for the state: it is their job to help people to function within society and to fit in without too much protest under the current regime, what we sometimes call the status quo. Remembering Ferenczi and his story, we might guess that even today therapists might know what it is to be silenced and to feel unable to speak about what they know. Valerie Sinason works as a psychotherapist with children who have been sexually abused and like Welldon she is employed under the National Health Service. In her essay 'Interpretations that Feel Horrible to Make and a Theoretical Unicorn', Sinason directly addresses this problem of feeling silenced.

Sinason's patients might seem to be the most vulnerable group possible, for these children are not only abused but they also suffer from physical and mental handicap. They might seem the least likely patients to have intellectual concerns. But she tells us that for these children it is a matter of the most intense anxiety that their experience should be correctly named and acknowledged by another person, as if to do without that naming would be yet another mutilation that they had to suffer. The point of the stories that she tells in her essay is to reveal that a strong counter-impulse can exist in the therapist, an impulse not to know, not to make sense, not to name. Sinason writes of an inhibition that comes over her as therapist, and as she suspects over other therapists, when she is brought face to face with 'a clear unbearable reality' which she is powerless to change. We might say ourselves that it is when she is brought up against the framework that she draws back.

The narratives that she relates tell of Sinason's own fear, which turns out not to be primarily one of hearing details that might disgust her, as some people might expect, but a fear of acknowledging what went on in the world outside her consulting room. Sinason explains that she used to feel that her training demanded, some unwritten law or some authority specified, that she should focus on the relationship between herself and her patients, not on what happened to them in the world outside. By the time she came to write the essay, she had already established that this was not in fact the case. But it was her interactions with her handicapped child patients that first taught her to see her own behaviour differently and to recognize that she was drawing back and refusing to name, refusing, in her own words, to link the inner and the outer worlds.

A deprived child who came to her for treatment cut up little pieces of white paper every week and poured them over a doll's face, saying 'erch'. For weeks, Sinason admits, she battled with 'interpretations' of what the child was doing instead of accepting it as a performance, a scene from the life of this child, in which she was using the doll to represent herself. When at last Sinason allowed herself to know, and to name, the child's response was almost bitter:

> Nervously, and feeling awful, I said hesitantly that perhaps the white stuff she was pouring over the doll was like the white stuff that comes out of a man's penis; I steeled myself for the response. She looked at me slowly and contemptuously. 'Well done', she said, starting a slow handclap. She knew.

'She had had to hold that experience herself until I could bear it', Sinason concludes. We have most have us heard about play therapy and that it can be easier for a child to demonstrate an action in play than to tell it in so many words. But this story seems to suggest another possibility, another way of reading the girl's behaviour. What if this intelligent girl was waiting for Sinason to name her experience, waiting for that as a permission, as the sign that she herself would be allowed to name what she knew?

The child's use of theatre and theatrical images, you might say, was calculated to draw language out of Sinason. When Sinason responded, uttering language, it was in the form of a comparison which links, not a label which demarcates, a comparison that joined the world of the play, the world of fantasy, with the outer world. The white paper was 'like the white stuff that comes out of a man's penis'. Without that naming, how could the child know that she herself would be believed and that what she knew and her very capacity for knowing would not be destroyed?

When as author Sinason wants to persuade her colleagues that they have been sharing her own inhibition, she finds herself in a predicament close to that of her young patient. She too is unsure whether her audience will be able to let her know what she knows, and she too turns to images summoned up by art. She quotes a poem by the German poet Rilke about the unicorn, one that she hopes will dissolve their resistance and mobilize what they already know:

> This is the creature there has never been
> They never knew it, and yet, none the less,
> they loved the way it moved, its suppleness,
> its neck, its very gaze, mild and serene.
>
> Not there, because they loved it, it behaved
> as though it were. They always left some space.
> And in that clear unpeopled space they saved
> it lightly reared its head, with scarce a trace
>
> of not being there. They fed it, not with corn
> but only with the possibility
> of being . . .

In Rilke's poem the claim not to know seems at odds with an intimate embodied knowledge, a knowledge that is both cherished and denied. That might remind us of Ferenczi's claim, that at the level of fantasy, people retain a memory of when they were treated with tenderness. Sinason makes use of the poem to tap this deep stratum in her readers. In the poem the physical presence of the unicorn, supple, mild-eyed, keeps reasserting itself, just as knowledge that is repressed is said to return.

Sinason chooses to ask her colleagues to consider a comparison. She repeats the poem here in the hope that her colleagues can recognize, as in a mirror, a confusion that she would suggest lies deep within themselves. They know but they won't allow themselves to believe that they know. Closer herself to the predicament of her handicapped patients than we might ever have imagined, Sinason too asks a set of images to carry meanings, to mobilize knowledge, via the body and the senses rather than the head. She too finds herself standing before an audience who are holding a knowledge that is buried and which they would prefer not to name.

In her essays 'Let the Treatment Fit the Crime: Forensic Group Psychotherapy' and 'Group Therapy for Victims and Perpetrators of Incest' Estela Welldon describes another way of working, an alternative to individual therapy, a way which specifically relies on the interactions between the members of a group and puts its faith in those interactions as crucial to recovery. She does not recommend this form of treatment for paedophiles, however, as these cases present difficulties all their own. Welldon's groups constitute societies in miniature, but the rules by which they are governed mark a departure from the rules of the world outside.

After thirty years' experience, Welldon writes that she began to understand what might be really effective in terms of therapy for these patients 'only when I allowed my clients to become my teachers'. Like Ferenczi, it was listening to her patients rather than any body of theory that prompted the method of helping them to which she turned. Accordingly, Welldon's position in the group is not one of authority as interpreter but like the other members she is there to listen and to respond. One of the things she listens out for are signs of danger, behaviour that frightens and agitates the other members. She takes it as one of her main functions to preserve safety in the room by calling a halt to frightening displays and to protect. It is in these circumstances that her clients meet, restored, as I would see it myself, to a secure world where their voices are positively required in order for their society to function, a world that duplicates in this respect the conditions that support development in early childhood.

Welldon prefers to treat both people who have been abusers and those who have been abused – though not ones who have been involved with each other – together in a group. Here, members whose positions are extremely polarized, psychologically speaking, are exposed to witnessing each other's experience and to interacting with each other. She also explains her choice in terms of the need to avoid reviving the 'stifling' dynamic of abusive intimacy, a word that has its own connections with silencing.

The stifling dynamic of which she writes is easily reawoken in one-to-one therapy, as she explains, where the therapist can be tempted, like the abused child who feels specially favoured, to believe that they are the only person who can help the patient; alternatively, they may find themselves playing out other roles as trapped child or dominating parent. Even though working in groups allows this deadlock to be avoided, however, she warns that the road to recovery is very long. Speaking for myself, it comes easily to read Welldon's model in terms of theatre and to see in it another way of mobilizing knowledge both for her patients and for herself. It seems to work by means of creating a theatre in which the actors are also members of an audience: this set-up means that interactions between participants can have the demonstrative power of a play.

Here Welldon has a special role. As I have been arguing, abuse damages the ability to think as well as causing emotional distress. Learning to think and to recognize reality is a huge issue for this group of patients: Welldon takes it as her own task in the group to 'offer links', to help her clients make the connections which constitute thinking. Abusers are observed to be unable to think, that is to interpose thought between experiencing their impulse to abuse and obeying it, while both abusers and abused can prefer to believe that there are no bad conseqences to their experience of incestuous abuse.

Sinason noted a reluctance to know both in herself and in other therapists, but in these clients, as Welldon prefers to call her patients, she finds a drive to self-destructive blindness that is more savage, one that she names as 'a tendency to make sadistic attacks on their own capacity for reflection and thought'. She has found that her own mind, too, has felt numbed and stupefied just by being in the presence of these wishes. It might be fair to say that such patients represent one end of a spectrum in which we ourselves, like the therapists, might also find a place.

In the group setting in which Welldon works, members learn to observe human behaviour that is close to their own in its patterns and to relate what they see to what they understand. Most powerfully, abusers find themselves confronted with the consequences of their own past actions, in the behaviour of other patients who have been abused. Welldon tells the story of one such encounter and of the shock of knowledge that was shared by all members of the group.

Keith, an 'old' or long-time member of the group, with a history of abusing his stepdaughter, indignantly challenged Patricia, a woman who had been abused when young and was still prone to meet her father's demands with compliance:

> Suddenly and quite unexpectedly a complete understanding of their own respective roles and of the implications was available to us all. We all became aware that incest is much larger than life, that its power is not only physical, sexual or erotic. This secret union provides both partners with a 'uniqueness' which it is almost impossible to describe. It gives as much as it takes away.

This may sound more mysterious than it really is, as comparison with a scene on stage can show. In this case, a well-grounded observation, made with some anger and calling for a return to realism, precipitated an insight that everyone present shared. Like a poem, though, it had to be experienced through the senses, words wouldn't do it, it was 'almost impossible to describe'. The whole group, actors and audience, as it were, were able to grasp a sort of identity-enhancing hyper-reality, one that many accounts have associated with the experience of incest. They found themselves in its presence without being bound by it.

Though it is acknowledged as a powerful reality by therapists, few attempt to offer any explanation for this compelling experience at the heart of incestuous abuse, one which was represented so vividly to Welldon's group. It is recognized as a phenomenon without any attempt being made to relate it to the world or to compare it with other features of social experience. Although she writes of her work very simply, it is clear that Welldon and her colleagues operate on a boundary where the most extreme emotional and psychological energies, to be compared with those obtained by splitting nuclear particles, are liable to break through.

That might be a useful way to think of what is going on here, for Ferenczi himself wrote of abuse in terms of a threat to the nucleus of identity when he was linking abuse with the power to know. Disrupted and disrupting as these energies are, they could nevertheless be brought into play in a form that was organized once Keith confronted Patricia in an act of conscious recognition.

For us as readers it is possible to go further and to attempt to make sense of the hyper-reality that incest seems or offers to confer. We might start by comparing it with the *amour folle* of an affair that is illicit, with its sense of heady triumph over the petty and contemptible, the escape from the everyday. We might go further and try thinking of it in terms of a hallucination, though not one that was completely random, a hallucination generated by the disrupted drive towards connection, a drive that, as I have been arguing, seems fundamental to human identity itself. That would both make sense out of something generally considered as extravagant and overblown and at the same time link it back with the world that is more familiar to us, the world in which children are raised and go to school.

Part II
On Being Reminded

Introduction

In the second half of the twentieth century artists were beginning to speak out about incest. Like time travellers or like those
awakening from sleep, for artists a new moment of coming to consciousness had arrived. Differing in kind from the voices of individual survivors, voices that were at that time still not publicly
acknowledged but shrouded in secrecy and guilt, these artists
offered their testimony on behalf of society as a whole. As if
finding themselves in a moment of recovered vision, they spoke
out on behalf of entire communities which had been traumatized
and silenced. None of the artists whose work I have chosen to
discuss here sets out, so far as I can see, with the principal aim of
presenting a study of sexual abuse. Instead they were engaging
with an attempt to explain central aspects of their own identities,
aspects which they associated with pain. They were asking about
their own suffering and how it had been created by their particular cultures and within the matrix of their own families.

Tennessee Williams, who told the story of a southern girl re-
scued from madness and of the death of her cousin Sebastian who
was gay, was himself a gay man from the south who had watched
his sister's collapse into mental illness. Ingmar Bergman, who
made his movie about a Swedish father who confuses his children
by pontificating on the subject of love while remaining emotionally absent, is the son of a Swedish pastor. The émigré Vladimir
Nabokov, who had to flee his native Russia for a wandering life
in Europe and the United States, had decided, as he acknowledged

to a friend, to write about a man with whom no one could identify, when he told the story of Humbert Humbert. It was in order to understand the ingrowing racial self-hatred of American blacks, as Toni Morrison the African-American woman explains, that she told the story of three little black girls on the brink of puberty. Arundhati Roy, whose story concerns the working through in one Indian family of the hybrid legacy of the colonized, where Christianity and Marxism are no less cruel in their effects than the rules of caste, is a highly educated woman from South India. The history of interaction between the Old World and the New, the shame of slavery and the burden of Christianity, have created problems of identity and perception for these artists as individuals, problems with which they have chosen to grapple in their work.

When they gazed out at the world around them looking for explanations, sexual abuse was part of what artists saw taking place there, and they heard this abuse often linked with the word 'incest'. They perceived a link between the notion of incest and other forms of abuse that were not sexual, recognizing abuse in all its forms as a manifestation of cruelty. These artists found that they had questions about the notion of incest, questions too about the loss of language and the loss of the power to know. Faced with what they saw for themselves, the links between education and abuse, between abuse and religion, these artists refused to be cowed and to look away. At the heart of the culture that separates out fathers, instead of a single taboo they registered a double ban: a ban on understanding our own experience and a ban on intimacy. Their protagonists struggle against an isolation and confusion which are presented not as personal failings but as systemic, the product of a specific history, the history of their families and of their communities.

The moment in which this clearing of vision began to take place can be aligned with the one in which Europe woke from the dream of Empire to find that the territories which it had appropriated were being reclaimed. Starting in India with Independence, which was finally retrieved in 1947, the political order began to shift on a global scale as one African nation after another took back sovereignty. No fewer than sixteen African nations became independent in 1961, the year in which the first film version of *Lolita* was being made. At a level deeper than they perhaps knew, artists were registering a supposedly private world of the psyche and a public outer world of politics which were not separated cleanly from each other but functioned in tandem.

As an end was being put to European colonization, some of those who had been educated in the traditions of Europe were making images of that other colonization, the one that takes place in the inner world, among the landscapes of the mind, when a regime that is alien is imposed by force. The works that I have chosen to explore here were created in the years between 1959 and 1996 as the old order of racial dominance shifted, allowing new ways of thinking to be entertained. It seemed to make sense for a start to choose movies and novels that were widely available. Apart from its historical grounding, my selection was also guided by the desire for breadth of range in the examples offered, both in terms of the human relationships examined and in terms of national origin and experience among the artists. But others would make different choices and there is nothing sacred about my own.

In this context it seemed crucial to include the voices of Toni Morrison and Arundhati Roy, as the voices of women whose people had taken the full impact of the colonizing power of Europe. In their novels which deal with incest, *The Bluest Eye* and *The God of Small Things*, losing self-respect and respect for the ways of one's own people, a loss which accompanies the experience of enslavement and colonization, is firmly connected with the motivation which produces acts of abuse. All the artists whose imagination gave birth to the stories examined here, whether that imagination was formed in the United States, Sweden, Russia or India, agree in offering a picture of the world in which one form of abuse that has previously gone unnamed is common and forms the foundation for sexual abuse and other forms of cruelty. They see a damage to the mind and spirit which touches every member of their society and is associated with teachings that are imposed in the name of religion, teachings which give a false picture of the world.

Like the child in Valerie Sinason's consulting room who waited to know whether she would be allowed to speak of what she knew, some of these artists were cautious and oblique as they made their own first moves. Showing abuse as part of a pattern, a thread that ran through, crossing history and geography, was going to be something new, something quite different from the old practice of representing relationships that were forbidden in order to tap into an eroticism that was intensified and charged. The film-makers chose to open the minds of their audience by first kindling their imagination through their eyes. These audiences were prompted, even stung, into asking questions: 'Are we really supposed to believe that Sebastian in *Suddenly Last Summer* was literally eaten?', one critic asked. These movies made people angry, because they brought them up against the bar on their own understanding. Part of the bewilderment, according to critics, seemed to be the whiff of 'incest': they used the terms 'incest' and 'incestuous' in their accounts of *Suddenly Last Summer* and *Through a Glass Darkly*, yet they could not help but register that these movies were each encompassing much more.

I begin by offering readings of the movies *Suddenly Last Summer*, *Through a Glass Darkly* and *Lolita*. These are something more than stories with a moving set of illustrations. As a medium, film allows the director to confront spectators with a world in which the marriage between word and image, which they are accustomed to expect, manifestly breaks down. Throwing viewers back on hearing language just as one form of sound among many others and confronting them with the part-objects and fragmented images of which cinema is made up – 'Hems of petticoats under summer dresses. Peeptoed shoes. Red toenails. Sandals' – the medium of film takes viewers back to an earlier form of perception, before they were taught where to look and how they should read. It reminds spectators that they are familiar with a different way of knowing.

The example of *Lolita*, however, which was first written as a novel, brings up the special problem for prose writers in approaching the topic of abuse. When groping for words, as so many voices heard in this book have shown us, educated usage gets in the way. After many attempts I myself found that the only way I could develop an argument on this topic which did not stall and come to a halt was by abandoning the usual forms of intellectual discourse and adopting the voice of the story-teller. Readers of *Lolita*, *The Bluest Eye* and *The God of Small Things* will notice that in each of these novels from the outset the writer makes a feature out of distancing the narrator's voice from the terms and usages of orthodox educated speech. In order to face the world squarely, in order to talk straight about incest, let alone think straight, each novelist leaves the schoolroom for the playground, turning received forms of speech to parody.

It is to mothers and to the part played by mothers that each of these creative artists returns. In the families imagined by the sons whose work I explore here the mother is either mad or dead – going on for both in *Suddenly Last Summer*, absent because she has already died mad in Bergman's movie. In tracing the psychological economy which gives rise to abusive acts, the works agree in giving a central place to mothers or to the mother-figures who are their symbolic equivalent. They present such older women as traitors, albeit inadvertent ones. The mothers who transmit a way of thinking that gives separate recognition to fathers – to fathers, we might add, who are white – create confusion: their children are abandoned as effectively as if the mother had died. For those women who as mothers choose the path of collaboration or who have been unable to resist indoctrination, madness and delusion are never far away. If they do not become mad themselves, the children whom they have abandoned will do so.

For the daughters, however, Toni Morrison and Arundhati Roy, in imagination, a mother who protects can be envisaged. The mothers who do protect their children, Claudia's mother in *The Bluest Eye* and Ammu in *The God of Small Things*, are also those who are close to men. It is with the steady beat of her parents' marriage in the background that Claudia is growing up. But in these imagined worlds the desire on the part of women for intimacy with a man is one that runs the risk of punishment. When Ammu, the mother in *The God of Small Things*, acts on her own desire and in doing so defies the system of caste, taking the Untouchable Velutha as her lover, first he, then gradually herself and over long years her children are destroyed.

In order to articulate their own inner world, the world of their imagination, and to set it in motion for an audience, all these artists start out from the same point, from the figure of a young woman. Rather than telling conventional love stories about her, however, it is on her mind and its confusion that they focus when they set out to tell the story of the daughter. Wondering about this concurrence, which it seems to me cannot be a matter of chance, I am brought back to the question of education and to the way that girls are taught to think. Instead of leading them out into the world, this education invades them, making prisoners of them. When their education invades girls with information, only some of which is explicit, about who they themselves are as young women, information that they feel upon their pulses to be false, those girls experience contradiction: it is this moment that artists take as their opening. It is with the challenge to a young woman's power of knowing herself and knowing the world that these stories begin.

Suddenly Last Summer
(1959)

On setting out my argument at the start of this book, I began by aligning with other forms of abuse the process by which girls receive their education. Speaking metaphorically and in terms of visual images this movie starts out from the same point, with its shots of a nameless young woman struggling as she is forcibly taken away for electro-convulsive treatment. Choosing to prepare spectators to understand the violence to which the minds of women are subjected was the decision of Gore Vidal, who was responsible for the screenplay expanding Tennessee Williams's original one-acter. In the play written by Williams all the action takes place in a drawing room. Vidal's expanded version, which was directed by Joseph Mankiewicz, adds scenes set in a hospital and in a convent, scenes which explore the ruthless pressure to give up the last of her independence of mind against which a young woman may be helpless, though in this story, for once, an exceptional young woman will be supported and her reason saved. This sympathetic account of young women and of their predicament provides a frame or perhaps a counterbalance to the portrait at the film's centre, which depicts Violet Venable, the monster-mother who in refusing to challenge the traditions and beliefs of her own southern culture betrays her son to his death.

In *Suddenly Last Summer* the scene opens on a sight that most of us would rather never see. Forget images of sexual intimacy about which so much fuss is made. Forget, for a moment at least,

physical violence, which can at least be kept at arm's length as
fantasy; in these opening images of the inmates of the female
recreation ward in Lion's Head hospital there is too much that
is familiar, too much that haunts us on the edge of vision,
especially for those like myself who have witnessed the breakdown of a mother. In the dulled and vacant faces, swept at
random by tides of cruelty or fear, the sly masks, the obedient
attention to rote tasks, alternating with bursts of fierce emotion,
we are shown, intensified, the craven, broken features of women
who have been unmanned. These women are in breakdown and
that in itself is terrifying but there is an added dread for the
audience in recognizing how close the women are, in play of
feature and behaviour, to the 'normal' women outside, women
still going about the lives that have brought their sisters to this
collapse.

   Dowdy clothes and unkempt appearance are part of the picture: in one sense this could be a prison, if it were not for the
uniforms of the nurses, which separate the 'well' women from
the 'sick' and remind us that this is a place of care, at least in
theory. The camera brings us back to focus on a young woman
we have already noticed playing with a doll, an image almost too
painful to contemplate. Is she a mother parted from her baby, a
woman longing to bestow her love, a woman who remembers
that as a little girl she once knew a place of safety in which to
play? She is not safe now, for as we watch, the nurses, like
warders, march her off, despite her struggles and cries, leaving
the doll collapsed and abandoned, like the living women who
remain in the room. The young woman will have electrodes
fixed to her temples and receive electric shocks at a high voltage,
a proceeding that would now be classified as torture if it took
place at the hands of the police. But there was a time in both
Britain and the US when patients who had been hospitalized
with breakdowns, my own mother included, were dealt with like
this. As the movie shows, the patient is, not surprisingly, sub-
dued in behaviour after receiving such violence at the hands
of those named as carers. Records show that there was usually
extensive loss of memory, that is to say measurable damage to
the brain was inflicted. For Tennessee Williams as for myself, this
was not a matter of abstract concern. In 1934 when his sister
Rose became disturbed she was forcibly given electric shocks, a

treatment from which her brother the playwright believed that she never recovered.

In the following scene of the movie we see a surgeon operating on a woman's brain, perhaps the brain of the very same woman, severing it one lobe from another, in a lobotomy, a procedure that was popular between the 1940s and about 1956 but was finally abandoned on the grounds that it obliterated the personality and the will. Some of us in the west are more used to thinking of the Soviet Union rather than the United States as the land where dissidents were silenced and punished in psychiatric wards, but this movie reminds us to think again. It suggests that the voice of a young woman bearing witness to her own experience might be a challenge to established views of the world, one so powerful that many would band together to silence it. In the United States, at the close of the 1950s, the most dangerous dissident of all might be a young woman.

The makeshift operating theatre set up in an old factory is falling to bits: the superintendent of the hospital is desperate to raise the cash for one that is purpose-built, where the brilliant surgeon he has lured to Lion's Head, Dr Cukrowicz, will be able to work on his new technique of lobotomy and make them all famous. A wealthy local woman, Mrs Violet Venable, has written to the superintendent, holding out an offer of funds, with the provision that the newcomer should carry out his operation on Catherine, her sick niece.

The setting in which the surgeon finds this lady, when he presents himself as directed, is theatrical but only in the pejorative sense that it is exaggerated and unreal, a world apart, cut off from ordinary life. Mrs Venable is lowered to greet him in an open elevator, styled in imitation of a throne, describing herself as a goddess who must descend. Played by Katherine Hepburn, she is doubly dramatized: her ferocious projection of herself and of her own view of the world is overpowering and quite without self-questioning. She takes over the young doctor as if he were a stage prop, pushing him around the set, all the while smiling and laying down the law with what she evidently believes is fascinating charm. The display shows us all too clearly what life must have been like at home for the son she is still mourning. Her son Sebastian died, she tells us, 'suddenly, last summer'. When she shows off the flesh-eating plant, one she has christened 'the Lady',

which she keeps in her jungle-like garden, we recognize that Violet
Venable too feeds upon flesh. If we were left in any doubt that
Mrs Venable was sick, we are shown her taking her medication.

Like Dr Cukrowicz, we too may be feeling shaken and overwhelmed, unable to place or name the energy Mrs Venable ex-
udes, though knowing that we feel excited by her presence. How
to place this excitement that arises in response to her glamour
and to her command of language? It could well be fear. She
holds both doctor and cinema audience transfixed by her horrify-
ing story of the baby turtles she once watched hatching in the
Galapagos, who were devoured as they made for the sea. We
can't escape from her and from her story, yet we aren't free to
respond to it exactly. When she reports that Sebastian had told
her he had seen the face of God when he watched the destruction of the little turtles, we are almost paralysed: we can't immediately summon the energy to remember the creature that feeds
on flesh who lives nearer home. It is only later that we might
think of asking whether Sebastian identified with the infant beings that could not escape and felt that he himself as a young
creature had been eaten up, the helpless prey of a mother whose
will was as inexorable as the will of God.

The movie helps us to understand our own response, by
returning to a more familiar sight. Unexpectedly the pair come
on another mother–son couple, the mother and brother of the
girl, Catherine, the one who is said to be sick. Catherine's own
mother does not share Mrs Venable's insistence on dominating
the proceedings, but in her stupid, greedy subservience she is
just as repellent. Catherine's mother is as eager as her aunt to
see her operated on: it is the price this mother will pay in order
to get the cash from Violet Venable that will secure an education for her son. Like the highly cultured Violet, who had asked
'What is a woman who has lost her only son? Nothing', Catherine's
mother has also learned to live in a man's world and accept that
it is her son that counts, her son that constitutes her own value
and gives her a place in the world. The name by which she
speaks of her own daughter is not Catherine but 'Sister'. In her
ordinariness, her frumpy, fussy fashion, this woman resembles
Foxy, Mrs Venable's secretary. They show us the everyday form
that is taken by the mania that we see in full exotic flower in
Mrs Venable. These are the women who do not go into hospital,
the ones who don't break down. But the film also shows us

how their minds work too and with that the price that others are made to pay: when Violet Venable had named her son Sebastian, she meant to yoke him to her just as in Shakespeare's play of *Twelfth Night*, Sebastian is the identical twin of his sister Viola.

Some critics complained that Montgomery Clift, who played the doctor, seemed confused and ill at ease, but for a young man in such company discomfort does not seem inappropriate and it gives our own anxiety a place on the screen. His next move is to visit Catherine, found by the camera alone in a bleak convent room. In the mansion, the primacy of cruelty in this culture was merely suggested by means of images, by the flesh-eating plant and other decorative features of the cultivated southern household: the picture of the transfixed St Sebastian, the life-size figure of a black slave and the flesh-and-blood black footman in his white gloves. In the convent, however, the consequences of this cruelty which has been institutionalized in the name of religion are played out in front of us. Unlike her female relatives, who were dressed with great care, Catherine is wearing a cheap ugly dress, of hard polished cotton that sits awkwardly on the curves of her body (plate 1). This time the warder we see in charge of a sick woman is in a different uniform; she is a nun and Catherine's bed stands under a crucifix. Among the symbols of sophisticated culture that abounded in her aunt's home, among the pictures and statues, was a death's-head angel figure, almost life-size, an image that links the wealthy mansion with the values of the convent. In the name of obedience, Catherine is dominated and refused all pleasure: when she snatches a forbidden cigarette, only to be told to hand it over, she is provoked beyond her endurance and in response grinds out her cigarette on the nun's palm. Refusing the masochism that is involved in obedience, Catherine too falls into cruelty, an act of cruelty that is likely to attract punishment, unlike the implicit cruelty that remains hidden in the form of images and unnamed.

It is from this spiral of disintegration that the young man who has come to visit will pull her back. First he excludes the nun, cuts out, as it were the middle man, the one who acts on behalf of an order that gives Catherine no value and denies what she knows. Catherine starts by angrily parroting the lies that have described her as mad and which asserted that she herself was lying when she claimed that a gardener made sexual advances to her (plate 2). (Watching the movie today, we have the benefit of

(Plate 1) *The warder with the crucifiix.*

(Plate 2) *The madonna comes between.*

knowing that in recent years it has become public knowledge
that within institutions sick and disabled patients are liable to be
made the object of sexual attacks.) For her, this repetition is a
way of keeping yet another potentially dangerous stranger at
arm's length. But once she is treated as an equal, given free
access to the adult pleasures that are symbolized, in this case – it
was a long time ago – by cigarettes, she will begin to admit to her
genuine difficulty. She is unable to remember or to remember
the whole story of what happened on the day when Sebastian

died. Her aunt, who prefers the story that her son the poet died
of a heart attack, had been affronted enough by Catherine's claim
that his death was violent; now the doctor discovers that she
knows that there are details which she is unable to recall. It
becomes the doctor's project to repair Catherine's mind rather
than to perform surgery on it, even though this brings him into
conflict with his boss, who wants to please Mrs Venable – like
a good son – and get her cash, to set up another institution
for fixing heads. At the level of imagination Violet Venable is
constantly presented as mother: one critic noted that when she
visits the superintendent's office, to press for the operation to
take place, the outfit she wears is cut like a maternity smock.
You could describe the doctor and Catherine as bad children, the
bad and disobedient children, however, of a mother who is being
revealed as monstrous in the way that she carries forward a tradition and a culture that bring only cruelty and death (plate 3).
Instead of using what he knows, his skill with a knife, to change
Catherine into a pliable, will-less creature, the doctor uses all his
skill to release her psychologically in order that she may say what
she knows. At a simple level, the tension of the film will come
out of the race against time that this involves, as the pressure on
him to operate mounts.

This involves first taking her out of the convent and putting her
in the nurses' home: stopping treating her as a madwoman, and
situating her among the sane, in effect. She is allowed to wear her
own beautifully cut clothes and to have her hair done; with this
her perfection as a choice and exceptional woman, a daughter of
the rich, is put on display, though we can't help noticing that the
black couture dress is as severe in its way and basically the same
shape as the schoolgirl cotton she was made to wear by the nuns.
But even in the hospital, Catherine is still not safe; her mother
and her brother visit her there to press her to submit to the operation that will change her for ever. As her aunt, who also comes face
to face with her there, puts it, 'What does it matter if she can't
think, so long as she is free of all that disturbance?', by which
Mrs Venable means that troubling, half-grasped knowledge, the
fragmented memory that disrupts Catherine's behaviour and chal-
lenges Mrs Venable's vision of her son. It is in the name of two sons
that it is proposed that Catherine, a daughter, should be sacrificed.

With what language could Catherine oppose her mother's
wheedling, her plea that Catherine should allow herself to be

(Plate 3) *See a pattern?*

mutilated? It is the movie itself that replies. The film shows her
running out of the room in fury and despair, only to find herself
trapped on a gallery, a walkway that crosses above the dayroom
in which the male patients spend their waking hours. We have
already been shown the stupefied potato faces of the women
inmates; the men we see are their brothers, their feature distorted by suffering in similar ways, reduced, like their sisters, to
compulsive activities like rocking or building houses out of cards
to manage their distress. Where is the important distinction between men and women here?

It would probably be difficult to shoot scenes like this today, as
we have come, for good reason, to be cautious about the way
sick people are represented. Yet I think it would be a mistake to
think that this movie is lacking in respect. Instead it might be
helpful to think of these scenes in the day room at Lion's Head

as scenes from a communal nightmare, a nightmare of what happens to the human when it is mutilated, stifled and confused.

A leering, brutalized sexual excitement spreads among the men in the ward, who cry out and lunge upwards towards Catherine as she stands in the walkway crossing high over the room. Her model-like perfection stands in grotesque contrast with their leers. Idealizing some women, setting them apart, as Taylor is presented here, held up in her couture dress and her perfect beauty, must perhaps lead to the ugly polarizing played out on the screen (plate 4). For a long moment the image invites us to recognize this division, one that cannot be distinguished from those created along the lines of class, and to register it as hideous. Mrs Venable had insisted on telling us how special she and her son were, how different from other people, how much more cultured and refined; the horrors underlying such a claim are now made clear.

A blond male orderly is the one who rescues Catherine: under instruction from Dr Cukrowicz he now injects her with a sedative. It is a procedure that we might be suspicious of today, but in this movie from the late fifties there is a trust in the power of the 'good' doctor, and a belief in psychiatric skills and techniques. When Catherine reawakens, though, it is to find that her aunt is in the room, and Catherine is again accused of lying. She runs from it again, this time to be trapped above the room full of deranged women, women who are not able to hide their derangement as her aunt does behind her elegance and her wealth. (By showing us the crossed Vs, though, on the panels of her limousine, aping the coat of arms on a coach, the movie does suggest that she was giving away a few clues. After all, 'delusions of grandeur' are a recognized symptom of mental disturbance.) But it is at this point that Catherine cracks; she comes close to throwing herself from the balcony in despair, falling into the deceiving mirror offered by the crazy women and half-drugged by their cries. It takes a man to rescue her; there has to be a man that she can identify with in order to escape.

This, it appears, is the part that her cousin Sebastian originally played: he offered her a means of escape. Before we learn how Sebastian met his death, it is Catherine's own story, we find, that the movie asks us to hear. The bait may have been a mystery, the mystery about Sebastian, but the crucial piece of information that we are asked to take on board is commonplace and presented with none of the frisson that accompanies Sebastian's story. Yet it is as

(Plate 4)   *Prison and separation.*

crucial to our understanding as the tale of her family's attempt to
get Catherine lobotomized.

Catherine was raped by a married man who had offered to
take her home when her partner got drunk at a ball. It was after
this that she had agreed to travel to Europe with Sebastian. As
she tells the story of this rape, sitting out in the exotic garden of
her aunt, Catherine brings into focus the everyday violence that

nobody has thought to mention when discussing her case. In the account she gives, of her wordless recognition of what was going to happen, of her helpless acquiescence, of the man's casual cue 'My wife's going to have a baby, we'd better forget about this', Catherine collapses an entire sequence of traumatic experience where body and mind were equally outraged and where the ground for further trauma was prepared.

When she went back to the ball and made a physical attack on the man who had raped her, nobody supported her or confronted him; Sebastian merely took her home. After this experience, she tells us, she started keeping a diary in which she referred to herself in the third person, a classic sign of dissociation, of splitting of the self. She took to staying in her room. It was this traumatized young woman that Sebastian firmly adopted as his travelling companion. Lacking any commentary from the on screen audience, it is left to us to wonder about his motives.

'I loved Sebastian', Catherine says. He was kind to her, buying her pretty clothes. But she also shows us that, like his mother, Sebastian used language with a brilliance that was attractive, even compelling, but at the same time heartless. Asked about Sebastian's father, we hear Catherine carrying Sebastian's voice in order to describe him. But when she hears her own voice utter Sebastian's phrase 'dull to the point of genius', Catherine hesitates. Now she hears the cruelty in his wit. Catherine too forms part of this world, where Sebastian's father was left at home to die uncomforted. Sebastian once took up residence in a monastery in Tibet, Catherine explains: to get away from his mother, as she says flatly. But Mrs Venable pursued him even there and stayed on till he consented to come home. We might be tempted to think that this is a picture of an isolated case, something freakish and out of control, or to lose sight of the way the story and the family we are watching are so carefully situated in an intensely cultured tradition, of which they are samples or demonstration models. But to understand the part that tradition and order play in creating this relationship between mother and son, we only have to remember Mrs Venable as she showed the doctor the garçonnière, the traditional room for sons of the family, the room where by her iron regime of pleasure Mrs Venable and Sebastian took their cocktails daily at five in the afternoon.

Critics did not fail to register that there was something bizarre in this relationship and they named that element as 'incestuous'.

When I first picked up that choice of words, I believed that any suggestion that Violet Venable's abuse of her son had ever taken a sexual form would be going much too far. But now I wonder. It is true that in 1959 'incestuous' was a term that was used more loosely, and offered the only language then available to describe a closeness that was excessive, one that excluded the outside world, as Violet Venable's hold on Sebastian sought to do. Yet in choosing this language, the critics were closer to a reality that usually remains unspoken than they could have known. Mothers as well as fathers have been known to abuse their children sexually, and the profile of Violet Venable offered by the movie matches with uncanny precision the profile of mothers who abuse. 'Incestuous mothers maintain a symbiotic relationship with their child(ren) and do not allow any process of separation and individuation', writes Estela Welldon in her essay on women who abuse. It is a problem that has been swept under the mat, in part, as she argues, because of the wish to idealize motherhood. What is left out of the picture according to Welldon is the way the experience of motherhood, with its almost total responsibility for children combined with total power over them, impacts on women. This idealization directly complements the idealization of masculinity and is equally dangerous and false.

As part of the system for maintaining the fiction that they are unlike men, women are discouraged if not prohibited from expressing anger, however difficult the situation in which they find themselves. Yet a deep sense of outrage may be at work below the surface in mothers, producing sadistic fantasies – we may think of the flesh-eating fantasies presented in *Suddenly Last Summer* – and dreams of revenge. As in the case of Violet Venable, there may also be a need to be in extreme control. These features may issue in sexual abuse of their own children in certain cases, given suitable circumstances, and a particular family history: Welldon writes of the triggering in a mother of the impulse to abuse as a process that involves at least three generations.

The movie offers Violet Venable and her world of southern culture as proud representatives of old traditions. Could it be that the secret at the centre of the movie, the secret about Sebastian that his mother can't bear to have told, really is incest? For Violet, any account of her son that differed from her own label – my son Sebastian Venable the poet – would be intolerable. But the stories about Sebastian and about herself as a daughter that Catherine reveals, when she is 'released' by the magic injection and encouraged by the good doctor, appear to concern something else, to reach out to making a wide statement about the world. Maybe Williams found as we have done that it was not possible to raise the question of incest without addressing an entire social order.

Catherine sits on the terrace, surrounded by all the other characters; like the detective at the dénouement of a murder mystery, she gives her report, she puts the pieces together. First she tells the story of her own rape, which led up to the trip she took with Sebastian. As she does so, her face and upper body flicker in and out of focus across the screen, making us experience the assault on her identity, the dissociation she is undoing by speaking. The idealized image of Catherine breaks down as she tells what she knows. When she comes to explaining Sebastian himself, however, she steps into confrontation with her aunt. Violet's interjections have to be silenced by the doctor as Catherine speaks into the reality of the relationship between this mother and her son. She names Violet's sickness and the ageing that was separating her inevitably from her son. Sebastian chose to find a different companion because he wanted a woman who was seductive, who would procure for him.

Sebastian was gay, something that his mother appeared not to recognize any more than she had recognized her function on his trips, the way he evaded her all-seeing eye. For Tennessee Williams, the playwright, who was gay himself, this information can hardly have been offered as a dirty secret: it is rather a clarification of reality. The movie has made us understand that a relentless identification with her was forced on Sebastian by his mother. This has made Sebastian both like her – he was a devourer of human flesh; 'Appetizing', he would say of the young men that he fancied – and with no taste for intimacy with women. It is not knowing that he was gay that has traumatized the matter-of-fact Catherine, so that for so long she could not string together a coherent account of his death.

What has silenced Catherine, over and above the attempts made from outside by members of her own family, her mother, her brother and her aunt, is the effect on her of witnessing her cousin's violent and unnatural death, coming as it did on top of her own psychological annihilation by means of rape. Critics complained about the end of this story; what, they said, could we be expected to believe that famished urchins had actually eaten Sebastian, that cannibalism was the secret of the film? The final minutes are taken up with a sequence in which the screen no longer asks us to concentrate on Catherine as she speaks about Sebastian but takes us back into showing the ordeal that they shared on the day when he died. The movie brings brother and sister, as it were, children of the same generation, and their fates, back into focus together. Working poetically by means of these images, it presents psychological truths about the way sons and daughters are mutilated, while also keeping the connection between them that the culture seeks to break. The movie has been suggesting all along that their fates, his death and disintegration, of which she is the silenced and traumatized witness, have been moulded by their culture as it was transmitted to them by its self-appointed representative, Violet Venable, the mother who knows that only possession of a son makes a woman worthwhile.

In this movie, at least, the daughter is heard when she speaks out at last. It offers an image of the frightening transformation that listening to her voice might bring, when before our eyes Violet Venable collapses into overt madness and is led away. In the garden, at last, only Catherine and the doctor remain. Here the movie encounters a problem that did not arise in the stage play, which closed on Violet's withdrawal. Was it Hollywood's specific demand for a romantic ending that prompted the awkward closure that brings Catherine and Cukrowicz together as future lovers? It is true that she has kissed him in the film and asked to be kissed, but those occasions seemed more like erratic boldness the first time and a demand for reassurance on the second occasion. There was a problem with the reputation of Montgomery Clift, the actor playing the doctor. 'Why aren't you married, Mr Clift?', journalists who knew he was gay had tormented him when he arrived to start filming in London. Though Elizabeth Taylor, his co-star and fellow-artist, made a close friend of him, outside the movie as well as on screen, it was still not allowable to admit that some men were homosexual, that homosexuality did exist as a part of ordinary daily life and was not some exotic taste of the depraved few. It is the pressure of that world, we must suppose, that brings Catherine and Cukrowicz at the close of the film to be positioned standing together, awkwardly and unconvincingly, as critics have complained.

These sequences towards the close of the film have prompted many hesitations on the part of critics. How can it be, they demand, that Taylor should become here the emblem of a desire that is homosexual? The oblique camera angles, the shifting shots

(Plate 5) *Black and white.*

offer deliberately incomplete and transient images of the crowd of young men behind the wire fence as they gaze, but who knows at what? Taylor in her swimsuit is presented as their focus but the camera itself lingers on the bodies of the young men. Was this the most explicit visual form that could be given to homosexuality in a wide-release film? Or is the point rather something to do with the likeness between homosexual and other forms of desire? One puzzle that some critics noticed was allied with this: in what sense could Catherine or Mrs Venable ever have been used as bait, when it was boys that Sebastian wanted to attract? We do know that women movie stars can become icons for gay men. In this movie, Catherine and Mrs Venable as wealthy women are given permission to care for their bodies and to present them in public, privileges of a femininity from which Sebastian and maybe other gay men too refuse to be separated.

Many themes are taken up and condensed or touched on briefly in this last movement. The history of relations between black people and white ones is a subject which it is still awkward to raise among white people in the American south. Yet it is a history that has structured perception for individuals on both sides. Towards the close of the film, that history is suddenly given focus after being glimpsed among such background images as the live black manservant in his white gloves, or the turbaned statue of the black serving man, which like the painting of a black man form the furnishings of Mrs Venable's home. Whiteness had been made salient from the start of the film, in the white uniforms of medical personnel and the white suit of Dr Cukrowicz, which is echoed by the white silk suit of Sebastian's that his loutish cousin makes off with. Mrs Venable's so-called maternity smock was also white. Now Catherine is shown wearing white, a white swimsuit issued by Sebastian that embarrasses her. Putting on this revealing white garment, she knows she is being used. His white suit is the only feature by which we are able to identify Sebastian himself, for we never see his face. The angel of death from his mother's house stands on the way to the place where he will be destroyed by the crowd of boys, poor boys, boys nameless and exotic, one turbaned, others banging makeshift musical instruments. Seeing the sequence out of context, it could look like a condemnation of the colonial past, a moment when revenge is taken on a white man by the brown boys who have accounts to settle with him (plate 5).

Through a Glass Darkly
(1961)

Out of the glittering waves of a sea that is black and white, words that promise a certainty that this movie is going to do its best to undermine, step four tiny figures. They are stick men, almost, like images from a child's drawing or a painting drawn on the wall of a cave. Only after a few moments is it possible to see that one of them is a young woman, the others male. It is the story of a young woman and her relationships with men, as they are defined within the family that we are going to explore. At the same time, we register her isolation from other women. The young woman who steps out of the sea is accompanied only by men; she is with her brother, her father and her husband.

She may be married but she has kept some of the ways of a child: it is with her younger brother that we first see her revealed as they go off together, skirmishing playfully as they run over the rough ground along the shore to fetch the milk. As viewers, we find ourselves caught up at once in the painful intimacy they share. The boy is in the throes of his own exigent sexuality, which has overwhelmed him and set him adrift from familiar emotions. He turns to his sister, confiding in her, and she meets him with tender concern: of course, she reassures him, there will be someone to find him attractive. But in no time at all the boy has also turned against her, attacking her on account of her sexuality, rather like a young Hamlet, angrily exclaiming against all women as he attacks the one who is closest to himself.

For a woman viewer at least, it is a disorienting moment: is this wan, rather schoolgirl figure that is his sister really to be taken as a heavy-breathing seductress? He is disgusted, he claims, by the sounds of love-making which he hears from the bedroom his sister shares with her husband. As viewers, we might interpret his response to such sounds, whether fantasized or real – a point I shall come back to – rather differently. We might ask about an envy and a desire in him that were only natural but for which he had no language, no means by which to know and accept what he felt. Was he frightened to be so drawn to intimacy with a woman? Instead out of his unrecognized feelings he manufactures an assault on the one whose body provokes them, the nearest girl. Out of this confused boy, what sort of man, what sort of husband and father will develop?

It is in the name of masculinity that the husband and father that the film wants to show us have gone off together, shivering. 'Masculinity demands it', they joke ruefully, as they put off changing into something warmer. The father, David, has just returned from a long absence and on this first evening at home the others have prepared a play for him. He is a writer, a very ambitious one, but when the boy self-consciously declares 'Of course father is a great writer', his sister's response is to burst into laughter. For us as viewers, any easy identification with either of them is disturbed. The girl's laughter is so wordless, so unattached. Could she be laughing at her father and his ambitions as well as at the boy with his pompous declaration; what does this youth know about great writing, we have to ask.

Meanwhile, Martin, the husband, who is a doctor, a man whose job it is to make people better, is giving his report on the young wife to her father as, wrapped in their dressing-gowns still, they steer their little boat among the reeds. She has just come out of hospital, it seems, and depends entirely on her husband now. He declares that he himself is all that she can cling to. He reports that his friend the psychiatrist, whom he trusts and who had care of his wife, has warned that she could have a relapse. Her dead mother, as we learn from her father at this point, suffered from the same illness, a sickness of the mind. This take on the young woman as utterly vulnerable and weak is unexpected: there was maybe something a little volatile in her, a touch wayward and intense, but she was no more unpredictable than her young brother. Is it only in contrast with the gravity, the weight of these grown men, who do not share her quickness, that it is felt as a little unsettling?

The unease to which we have been introduced does not let up, for as the supper which precedes the play goes on, it is clear that this father brings disappointment. It emerges, but only under his children's close questioning, that he is not going to keep his word and stay with them but is intending to set off again soon on yet another trip. He is going to act as a guide in Yugoslavia, this man who does not seem to know much about his own children. The presents he has brought for them, and for the husband who is by marriage and according to generation also his child, are ill-considered: he picked them up at the airport at the last minute, they can tell. Yet when the camera follows the father into the house where he has gone to search for his pipe, as he claims, it reveals him weeping bitterly, a desperate man, trapped in isolation and unable to put his grief into words or to share it with these others.

His children want to tell him what they know about him, but they do not speak directly. Instead they present it in the form of a play, a play for which he and the cinema audience with him are the sole spectators. Brother and sister speculated in their walk, recalling his former mistress; now they put on a play, a mock-heroic one, almost like the play in *Hamlet*. Naming their drama 'The Artistic Haunting', they present a story of betrayal followed by an attempt to evade the knowledge of guilt by turning to art. The daughter in a flowered robe and mantilla takes the woman's part while the son in a false moustache swaggers and struts (plate 6). But the part the girl is playing is the part of a ghost: the speaker explains that she died in her thirteenth year. The signal is an oblique one. The husband also takes part; sitting at the side of the stage he strums an accompaniment and fails to be disturbed.

The play seems to have failed: that is, the father who is the audience offers wooden applause, but he does not seem moved or to have been made to think. Although 'the play's the thing / Wherein [we'll] catch the conscience of the king' in *Hamlet*, here it does not remind the father of anything in himself or in his own life. His son, who wrote the play – it turns out that he too wants to be a writer – is defeated by his father's refusal to respond and reacts by accusing not his father but himself: his little play was 'crap'. The boy is growing up palpably but he is also losing something: last year he could stand on his hands and walk on

(Plate 6) *Speaking out, but under a veil.*

them as easily as on his feet, but this year he can no longer get his balance. We are watching him as he loses connection with his body and gives up belief in himself. By the end of the movie he will be an uncritical worshipper at the father's shrine.

It is still light outside: for most of Europe, this Scandinavian lightness, these white nights of summer, are exotic. Now we see the married couple in their bedroom. If the brother heard sounds of passion from in here, he must have been dreaming, for it is clear from the wife's apologies – 'I'm sure I'll want you again in that way some day' – that sexual passion between them has shut down. The intimacy that is promised to the viewer by the sight of the large, handsome actor in his pyjamas somehow stalls: the wife apologizes, the husband addresses her as 'Little Karin', as though she were a child. His patience absorbs any latent energy that threatens to be ignited by their interactions. Sadly she looks at him: 'You always say exactly what is right don't you? That is why it is never right.' Though the husband may think that he is handling a delicate case with professional skill, to the audience it can look as if he were refusing something, withholding himself. Perhaps that is one source of Karin's sadness: the language which is available to this family is one that cannot carry feeling. It is left to the lonely voice of a cello, sounding a movement from Bach's second suite in the background from time to time, to speak of longing.

Karin can't sleep that night: neither can her father. He had said he would clear up the supper things and then work at his writing. Getting out of bed, she wanders in to the room where he is seated at his desk, solemnly trying out phrases, all of them rather dull, aloud. She sits herself on his knee, as though she were a little girl. From what moment, I ask myself, did we begin to feel that this family was somehow off-key, a little weird? There is nothing sexual in the interaction, no demonstration of erotic response, and yet the position is one associated with sexual play. Or with tenderness between an adult and a child. It is not a pose that a father and his daughter, once she is a grown woman herself, and married to boot, could take up without awareness of its sexual dimension. But perhaps Karin is retreating into the world of the little girl that she once was in the time before the trauma that produced her mental illness took place. Past and present overlap for us as we watch the dreamy, sleepwalking face of the young woman and the closed, tight-lipped, hatchet visage

(Plate 7)   *Without speech.*

of the father, who is so distant from her now. When he lifts her
onto his own bed and tucks a blanket round her, she sighs 'Like
you used to', falling briefly asleep (plate 7). Maybe it is to Ferenczi
that we should turn for an explanation of Karin's behaviour: he
described something very like it when he observed that at the
level of fantasy abused children retain the memory of tenderness.

    Karin shares other characteristics with people who have been
abused: she is incapable of approaching her father directly. Like
the play, this sleepwalking scene fails; the father does not take
her cue, he neither asks what she is doing nor acknowledges that
it might have meaning for him too. He is stonily impassive in the
face of this second cautious signal, this attempt to make contact with him and to acknowledge the past. It is not surprising
that Karin's sleep cannot last. Restless, she moves on out of the
inhabited part of the house, up into the attics and the empty
rooms where nothing but the now invisible past still lingers.
Noticing that the peeling wallpaper is patterned like the dress
that Karin wore to play her part, as viewers we take the cue
which links this scene with the earlier scene of the play. There,

what she so deeply knows that she cannot get rid of it, the knowledge she cannot divest herself of, confronts her. In the form of
whispering voices, of faces half glimpsed behind the patterns of
the wallpaper, what Karin knows and cannot lose but also cannot
get acknowledged by her father rounds on her in an attack. The
film has taught us to understand something that escapes both her
husband and her father, that Karin's illness is not a random mis-
fortune but is linked with the past and with her father, linked
too with a thwarted drive to name and understand. Thwarted in
her, at the same time, as a grown woman, is her sexuality. She
has lost her desire.

Next day the two older men take the boat off together, to get
provisions, leaving brother and sister alone. Karin is supposed to
be helping Minus with his Latin, a holiday task from school that
he has brought away with him. For Karin's brother, too, though
in a different way, desire and relationship are problems; behind
his textbook or under it, he has a girlie magazine. The really
urgent subject for both of them is one that has attention diverted
away from it, in the name of education. Perhaps we are as uncomfortable as Minus when his sister joins him in looking at the
pin-ups: it would be easy to say that it's not a suitable activity for
a young married woman, but let's resist that simple answer. Aren't
we brought up by this sequence against the troubling question,
one that we don't know how to answer, of what form the desires
of Karin herself now take? The magazine claims to show what
men want in a woman. It is possible that for Karin the keenest
desire of all is to be allowed be fully herself and to voice what
she knows.

It may be too late, however. The sun is hot: Karin takes her
brother inside. Offering to show him something special, she leads
him up to the attic rooms where she sees, projected onto the
walls and into the silence, the knowledge that she cannot put
into direct speech. Instead of speaking to Minus of the event, the
story that we shall never hear told but that hovers, like the faces,
just out of focus, she gives up the attempt to make contact
through the language of theatre or of mime, and instead attempts
to share what she knows with him by positioning him alongside
herself. Instead of giving her perceptions external form, she offers to draw Minus into her inner world, where they are played
out as hallucination, projection, images and voices that animate
the space around her in which she is isolated.

Appropriately alarmed, Minus recoils, leaving Karin in despair, her last hope of an audience destroyed. It is in this despair that she hurls herself out of the house and takes refuge in the hull of an old wreck where her brother later finds her, shivering and sodden under the onslaught of a storm that this makeshift shelter cannot keep off. With this final failure of her attempt to share what she knows, Karin's inner world has collapsed. Tenderly, finding that he cannot move her or bring her back to herself, her young brother fetches coverings to keep her warm (plate 8). It is in the presence of that tenderness that a coupling takes place between brother and sister, a coupling that is only fleetingly implied but was picked up by those reviewers who did name incest in connection with this film.

(Plate 8)   *The Pietà reworked.*

But it seems that a sexual encounter with her father, one that has had long-term effects, may be the unspoken secret that has wrecked Karin's mind. A little later we see her father as he takes his turn in watching over Karin in the wreck. In contrast with Minus, he does so from a distance and without attempting to offer her comfort, as if he were her warder (plate 9). Seeing this absence of tenderness, we are reminded of the father's distress in his own isolation, a distress which was revealed earlier in the movie when he wept. In real life, as we have learned, Father Porter's response to his own isolation as a father was to use his superior power to get intimacy on sexual terms. Is this a solution that David, as Karin's father, turned to when her mother died, the secret that Karin is unable to utter?

It is on her father and his shortcomings that the film now turns. Karin's husband bitterly accuses this father of total selfishness, yet the father meanwhile speaks about love, glibly as he wrote about it in his novel. Neither seems to be using the right language. The father's tone is pious here, and full of mystification: what he says does not add up. Martin, Karin's husband, has been accusing him of heartlessness and of flirting in his writing

(Plate 9)   *Together in the wreck.*

with ideas of God. David answers him by speaking of his own recent failed attempt at suicide: 'Out of my emptiness something was born which I hardly dare touch or give a name to. A love. (Pause) For Karin and Minus. And you.' For the audience, it is an invitation to scepticism if we can only allow ourselves to believe that a serious older man, saying such apparently praiseworthy things, is open to criticism, or if we can allow ourselves to wonder what it is that he has to reveal when he says tantalizingly: 'Maybe I'll tell you one day. I don't dare to now.'

For many viewers, including its first critics, this was not a move which they could make. They never dissociated themselves from the authority of the father and of the Christian religion for which he seems to speak. At the close of the film, when Karin has been airlifted away to hospital, the father speaks to his son, saying, as if drawing the conclusion from the sequence of events we have all witnessed, 'God is love.' Instead of taking up the cue offered here and asking for themselves about the exact relevance such a pious statement had to the suffering shown in the film or to its events, reviewers apparently shrank from pointing out how absurd it was as a comment, when taken simply at face value. They did not link it with the title, *Through a Glass Darkly*, with its quotation from St Paul about imperfect vision, or ask about irony on the film-maker's part nor did they wonder about confusion. Instead they went along with the father and his pious voice. Like young Minus, uncritically grateful for the attention, who cried joyfully 'Father spoke to me', reviewers stifled their own impulses of scepticism.

That is something that Karin was not able to do and that we are not obliged to do ourselves. When we last see her in the film, Karin is elegantly dressed, and has resumed an identity that we never knew was hers, the identity of a fashionable young urbanite. For a moment we see that, like Catherine in *Suddenly Last Summer*, Karin has been asked to project an idealized image of herself as a woman. What we ourselves have been watching, however, is the disturbed young girl hiding under the shell of perfection. Reversing the journey made by Catherine, Karin has asked to go back to the hospital from which she had been so recently released: 'I can't live in two worlds any longer', she explains. And which are these worlds? The world as she knows it herself, and the world as it is named by other people? Before her resolution is taken, at the point where her father and her husband return to

(Plate 10)   *Fighting for her life.*

find brother and sister huddled in the old wreck, Karin gives her most frightening display of disintegration. Up in the attic rooms again, wild, resisting her husband's attempts to calm and bring her under control, she insists, theatrically, 'He's coming, he's coming (plate 10).' No one in the film, or so far as I know outside it, pays sufficient attention to ask her who is coming, or rather, who once came and why Karin should be afraid of him. If those questions were raised, we might ask ourselves whether she was making yet another attempt to tell her story, by acting it out before her husband, acting out the scene of a trauma that the movie repeatedly points to but, like Karin herself, does not spell out.

Watching her wrestling, struggling against the confining embrace of a man and making use of the word 'coming', I am reminded once more of Valerie Sinason's young patient. Like that young girl Karin speaks in code. 'God is a spider', Karin tells her husband, her verbal language moving ever further away from direct report. Who hides behind the name of God, whose touch is more unwelcome than a spider's? The movie itself stops short here but we are free to break the silence in which the history behind Karin's breakdown is entombed. It might be better described as papered over, since the working title for the film when it was under production was 'Wallpaper'. Following Sinason's example, we might take Karin up and venture to reframe her communication more directly: that struggle she puts up, with her speech in which God and spiders are mixed up, looks like an attempt to defend herself against a past rape by her father, when his powerful limbs seemed to be everywhere, like a spider's, when he used both arms and legs to pin her down.

Lolita
(1962 and 1997)

Looking back, Humbert realizes what he did to Lolita, when he hears the voices of children rising from a playground in the valley below. 'From those voices, the voice of Lolita would be missing forever', he laments. Early in Nabokov's novel, in a scene which was picked up in both the 1962 movie and the 1997 remake, finding herself alone with her stepfather in a hotel room where there was only one bed, it was Lolita's voice which named the act to which her stepfather was leading: 'The word is "incest"', she said. That bold shot was her last. Their life together, a life which was established on Humbert's terms and was shaped only by his needs, was one from which she could not escape. Her mother was dead. 'She had nowhere else to go', as he put it himself. Months down the line, Humbert, in his role as the good father, was trying to coach her in order to improve her tennis, when he realized that Lolita had lost the ability to play an attacking game. We ourselves are able to recognize what that means in terms that are less figurative, when we contemplate the poverty and ugliness which she later came to choose through her marriage. After Humbert, Lolita could no longer put herself out there and play the game of life in order to win.

The novel first came out in Paris, with Olympias, who were known for publishing pornography. The first notice taken of it in the *New York Times* was a dismissive one as a result. But once Harry Levin, well-known critic and Harvard professor, had written a letter in the book's defence, which the *Times* then published, saying that the novel was a work of literature, American publishers vied to bring it out. 'I challenged myself to find the person that nobody would be willing to identify with and to write his story.' So Vladimir Nabokov explained his project in writing his novel *Lolita*, to his friend Elena Levin. He had chosen to speak about something which sounds close to the absolute isolation which we have come to associate with ideals of masculinity. In doing so he found himself also involved in chronicling how a seemingly perfect man – both the actors who have played Humbert, James Mason and Jeremy Irons, were stunningly attractive and specialized in high-status parts – recognized a soulmate, not in adult women but in a young girl. Humbert shares something of the vision of adult women and of mothers that *Suddenly Last Summer* and *Through a Glass Darkly* have sketched out. His own mother, like Karin's, is dead. Lolita's mother, who plays such a central role in the early part of the story, in her vulnerable and provincial way is as keen on allying herself with culture as Violet Venable. In his novel Nabokov is careful to frame Humbert's story by showing first the loss of his mother, when he was a young teenager, and then, swiftly following it, the loss of his first sweetheart. Finding Lolita, he tells us, is like finding once more his own first explorations of intimacy with a woman and with her body at the time when, like Laurent in *Murmur of the Heart*, he was on the cusp of adolescence, an experience that for Humbert is tied forever to loss.

But Lolita is not the first little girl who has provoked these sensations for him, as Humbert makes clear. She is merely the one who will be the last, the one with whom he will act out his fantasy of completely secure and unchallenged possession. According to many therapists, compulsive behaviour is always linked with the inability to mourn. From the outset, the novelist frames Humbert's obsession with Lolita as compulsive and as a repetition, a symptom that he connects quite specifically with the death of Humbert's mother and of her surrogate, his first love. In failing to transmit that vital cue, the 1962 movie sells its audience short. Rather than this cycle of tenderness, it is within a cycle of violence that the story is positioned by the 1962 film. That opened with James Mason on his way to destroy the man who 'stole' Lolita. But in the opening of the 1997 movie, a desperate or despairing mix of violence and tenderness, one that we ourselves can recognize, for it has repeatedly presented itself when we have approached the topic of sexual abuse, takes on visual form. We see this cycle

(Plate 11)   *Direct and unafraid.*

embodied in the figure of Jeremy Irons, his face streaked with blood and with tears, clutching at a kirby grip as he drives one-handed, his car lurching all over the empty road.

Lolita is the story of a very young girl, one on the brink of sexual discovery of herself, very much as Laurent was in Louis Malle's film. In casting Dominique Swain as Lolita, Adrian Lyne was faithful to Nabokov, who set Lolita's age at twelve, disturbing as this made the movie – even more disturbing than when the part was played by Sue Lyon, who was older and looked it. I ask myself about this disturbance, wondering whether that moment in a very young girl's life is conventionally one from which we have agreed to turn away (plate 11). That could make it seem as though it were not decent. Are we made uncomfortable, as an audience, or as readers, by being confronted with something that we did not know about, something unnamed or untamed? In grown women, the outspokenness of the child, her clarity, is not usually allowed to live on and enter into alliance with a sexual magnetism. But in Lolita we see a twelve year old who is already curious about sex and about the power of her own body, even though she may look and behave like a little girl. The contrast between Lolita and her mother, between Lolita and any other grown woman seen on screen in either version, is powerful. It invites us to pursue the recognition that there is something wrong with what girls are asked to become, something false. Watching Shelley Winters as Lolita's mother can be positively agonizing for any woman of my generation; she is made so transparent in her suburban pretensions, so patently undesirable and smothering, so urgent for sex. That early movie identifies with Humbert's distaste much more uncritically than the 1997 version. Coming after the women's movement, that version was made in a world where it was easier to see Charlotte, Lolita's mother, more generously. Lyne cast Melanie Griffiths to play her with both more glamour and more dignity.

What remains troubling, in each movie, is the relationship between mother and daughter. Her mother treats Lolita – 'my little Lo' – with a lack of respect that would be surprising if it were not painfully familiar to many women. She speaks to her as if she were a servant, or someone she deemed less worthy than herself, rather than her own daughter. It is as if she did not expect to find so did not look for any way of expressing her love. In this situation, it is hardly surprising if Lolita makes an alliance with Humbert, the man who comes to live with them, the new lodger.

The story told originally by Nabokov takes the form of a confession, a statement purporting to have been written in prison, by Humbert Humbert, who recounts the tale of his relationship with Lolita, a young girl who is thirteen when he first makes love to her. Having caught sight of her lying in the garden, he agrees to take a room in her mother's house. Humbert is a college professor, come to take up a post in a small town. The mother finds him attractive, never suspecting the erotic excitement roused in him by her young daughter. Lolita, whose father is dead, as Jennifer Montgomery's may be and like Catherine's in *Suddenly Last Summer*, welcomes the advent of Humbert, flirting with him, testing to see how far he will go in his sexual play with her, and makes an alliance with him, as a rebellious teenager, against her mother. In order to secure the right to stay near her Humbert yields to the mother's pressure and marries her, moving into the position of father to Lolita, a position that is never incidental to his relationship with her.

He can barely tolerate his new wife, this wife who is also a mother, drugging her in order to escape her sexual demands (plate 12). He is already fantasizing about killing her, and has armed himself with the gun which had belonged to her first

(Plate 12) *Who's Mummy's boy then?*

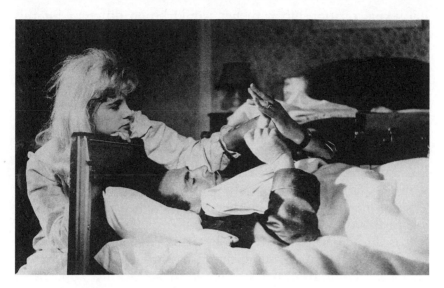

(Plate 13) *Lolita's the grown-up?*

husband, when she breaks into his desk, in her frantic push for
an intimacy that she rightly suspects he is withholding. There she
reads the diary in which he records his passion for Lolita and the
disgust that he feels for her mother. At this point the scales fall
from her eyes and her blindness is over. Weeping, enraged, she
writes the letters that are designed to expose him and to cut him
off for ever from contact with her daughter. As she runs out in
the rain to mail them, she is knocked down and killed. His
fantasy of her mother's removal fulfilled, as Lolita's father
Humbert will now have sole rights of access to the daughter,
rights that are unlikely to be challenged.

Her mother had sent Lolita off to summer camp, planning that
she should not return home but move on from there to a school
designed to break her spirit, a religious foundation. Instead Humbert
picks her up from camp and drives her to a luxurious hotel, claiming that her mother is sick. That is the moment when Lolita names
his intentions and utters the word incest. That first night they sleep
in separate beds but the next morning, resuming her sexual play,
she offers to show him the games she had been learning at camp
(plate 13).

Humbert makes no resistance to this, deceiving himself, as we
may feel in our role as listeners, when he claims 'I was not even
her first lover.' He speaks as though his entering into a full gen-

ital sexual relationship with her would be no different for this thirteen year old from the experience of exploring her sexuality with the teenage boy at camp. He's so jealous of this teenager that the sophisticated Humbert doesn't see anything odd about viewing an awkward boy as a competitor or suspect that it is the boy in himself that is in the driving seat. Like Lolita's mother, this stepfather too is blind. His blindness permits him to read the situation as one in which he, not the young girl in his care, is the one who is naive and exploited. He identifies so intensely with Lolita that he is not so much having a relationship with her, which would require both parties to be separate beings, but using her as a mirror image; in a sense Humbert wants to be Lolita, to reclaim what is his own that he sees in her.

It is during their stop at this hotel, the Lonely Hunters, that the figure in the background, the man who will haunt this story and 'steal' Lolita from her stepfather, makes his first appearance in disguise. Like Humbert, we have already met him, back in Lolita's hometown. Quilty was a writer, a man whom Lolita's mother had pursued: this figure has so much in common with Humbert that Nabokov makes it easy for us to think of Quilty as necessary to the story, as not just parallel to Humbert but as a figure acting out what Humbert knows, his own guilty awareness that is being suppressed, a guilt that could separate him from Lolita.

Humbert wants to see himself as a good father to Lolita at the same time as he wants an active sexual relationship with her. How can this confusion arise? When Kubrick chose to show the hands of James Mason plying a tiny brush loaded with nail polish for the toes of Sue Lyon behind the opening credits of his movie, he brought into focus Humbert's longing to be associated with women: at the same time Kubrick reminded his audience that this longing would normally have been absolutely blocked. Only by standing in for a woman, taking the place that is usually reserved for a girl-friend, could Humbert or any other man achieve the intimacy with a girl that is open to girls among themselves. As a man, it might be that Kubrick recognizes Humbert's longing, without sharing that personal history of traumatic loss that produces Humbert's compulsion. Not everything about Humbert is out of whack.

The desire for intimacy with girls, on terms that are not sexualized, for recognition as it were, as one of them, marks a wish to steer clear of falsehood, the falsehood that is imposed on adult women in the name of femininity. In Lolita Humbert has found a girl who has not yet been taken in by the orthodoxy that is offered to her by her mother. Unlike this mother, with her constricting clothes and her high heels, Lolita is still connected to her body, enjoying the feel of the warm grass beneath her and the water-sprinkler over her back as she lies in the sun (plate 14). She is unselfconscious about the braces on her teeth – those braces that in the 1997 movie oblige us to keep registering that she is under-age – uncritical of her body and of herself: rude and difficult, as her mother names it. She is testing out the world as she moves beyond the edge of childhood. This openness to the pleasure of being alive is recognized by Humbert, an openness that is seen in none of the adults. It is this that her mother wants drilled out of her, though in this she is clearly meant to be no different from other mothers, but indeed recognizably the same.

In Humbert's imagination, there is no connection between mother and daughter: he separates them from one another in his mind (plate 15). But his fantasy did not correspond with reality in this respect. Once he has had sex with Lolita for the first time, he tells her that her mother is dead and is shocked, as we may be ourselves, by the agony of weeping that overtakes the young girl. She mourns fully and helplessly. But now she is entirely in Humbert's power, he can believe that she 'belongs' to him as he has dreamed that she will and now he alone will determine the shape of their lives. This compensates him for the danger of moving so close and taking the risk of renewed loss. It means, as we see very quickly, that he takes over where her mother left off, in the sense that Humbert now becomes tyrannical in what he imagines as his attempts to be the good father. Though Lolita is bright and sassy as they travel in the car, as an adult he can find her chatter irritating and want to correct and control her. Eventually he will come to the point where he strikes her across the face. From this act of silencing, we watch him move on to rape. Far from being a story about love, as some critics have claimed, *Lolita* tells about a mounting violence.

Humbert tries to make sure that Lolita has no money of her own, partly because he is afraid that with independence she will make off, a possibility, as we find much later, that she has kept open for herself. All the time she is with Humbert she is also in touch with Clare Quilty, as he tails their car. In the long, dream-like passage from motel to motel across America, a passage that traces a continent and the lives of all those it contains, the

(Plate 14) *In comparison, Humbert's a ghost.*

(Plate 15) *Separation between mother and daughter.*

dynamic of this relationship is played out over and over again before the audience. We watch Lolita learning to exploit in her turn, when with a turning of tables that is pitiful she assumes authority and insists on payment item by item for the sexual tastes that she divines and gratifies in Humbert. We see the boredom with which she responds to Humbert's physical arousal: 'Not again', she groans. What member of the audience could feel that Lolita is abandoned to pleasure or corrupted by it when they see her servitude, her scrabbling for coins, her weeping as she lies awake at night? As she learns to manipulate Humbert and to practise deception, she is losing what she knew about pleasure and what she knew about how to live.

This may be what they pick up at the fancy school in which Humbert, in his role as the good father, enrols her, once the autumn comes and they settle down so he can take up his post as a college professor. Where Lolita's mother was linked with the church, her stepfather, the college professor, is linked with education, but the movie suggests a close tie between these two institutions. 'Humbert the happy housewife', Nabokov makes him write: and in Kubrick's film he is seen wearing an apron, cooking dinner. At this point in the movie Lolita is restored to a home set-up that is surprisingly close to the one in which we first found her. Humbert now tries to control Lolita by the sort of nagging and close supervision that her mother used to employ (plate 16). In a sense we are being reminded of the hidden part in ruining her that was played by the ordinary way that girls are bullied in the name of training them as they grow up. In spite of his attempts to turn her into the model schoolgirl, it is recognized that all is not well with Lolita and the headmistress asks to speak with her father.

If we hoped that this signals exposure for Humbert and for Lolita escape, we can think again: the school too is blind. They want to talk to Humbert about Lolita's failure to take an interest in boys, for that, the headmistress claims, is one of the foremost aims of the school: turning out girls who date. Lolita seems to be a bit slow in that department. Choking on his piece of cake, Humbert assures this woman and the clergyman who sits at her side that he has the matter of Lolita's sex education in hand. At that moment, as audience, Nabokov cuts us free from any identification with the school. Lolita is indeed isolated and without help among these adults.

(Plate 16)   *A teenager with something to be angry about.*

This part of the story seems like a replay, in fact, a way of showing how a girl in circumstances that are more ordinary, even normal, could be bullied and crushed. Lolita's seclusion, the veto on her joining in with others her own age, has much in common with the story of many girls brought up in families where there is a great mistrust of the outside world, ostensibly on moral grounds. Only with enormous difficulty does Lolita obtain permission to take part in the school play: at the dénouement we will learn that this play allowed her to meet more openly with the man who was its author, Clare Quilty, and who is the means of escape she had been keeping open for herself.

His jealousy and the fear that Lolita can be 'stolen' from him by some boy make Humbert desperate to limit her freedom, so that when he finds that she has been deceiving him, claiming that she was at piano lessons, he is beside himself. Yet another violent scene between father and daughter ends in her leaving the house, in an abortive attempt at escape which does at least

allow her to make a plan over the telephone with Quilty. We
have been watching not only the deterioration of the relationship
but also the imminent collapse and disintegration of Humbert
himself. This will finally be completed when we see him face to
face with Quilty, recognizing him for a moment as a man who
has split himself.

When Humbert and Lolita set off together for the second
time, though he is not consciously aware of it, she has arranged
that they will be followed by Quilty. At some level, though,
Humbert does know, and the pressure of this knowledge is
reflected in the pain that he feels in his heart. Lolita too is sick,
as we have learned to register, given to deception as a way of life,
a way of survival, linking intimacy with tyranny, and hostile. In
this she is not so far from Humbert himself. Once she found
herself trapped, she never stopped resisting her stepfather and
planning to get away. Lolita's sickness is registered in total collapse, with a case of flu. This lands her in the hospital from
which Quilty rather than Humbert will take her home. Humbert
now finds himself abandoned to accelerating collapse, which first
takes the form of sickness like Lolita's, then of a complete loss of
inhibition as he attacks the medical staff who let her go.

From here it is only a blink to the end of the story, the closure
that will only arrive once Lolita gets in touch with him some
years later, to show what he has made of her. In the meantime,
true to his compulsion, he has traced and retraced the paths of
America, looking for her. Finding her again, he discovers the
Lolita he shaped for himself in a young woman who approaches
him asking for money. What he hopes of this meeting is that she
will come back to him: instead of this, he has to learn, as we
do, the story of Lolita's association with Quilty and of her disappointment in him. Quilty wanted to film her in group sex
for his porno movies: he tried to take the dominance imposed
by Humbert one stage further, and she left him. 'I really loved
Quilty, he was the only man I ever really loved', she exclaims,
with apparent guilelessness, in a move that shatters her father
and might well take us aback. But we have to ask ourselves how
much we know about Lolita by now; she had masked herself and
what she wanted for so long, does even Lolita herself know what
she might want apart from revenge?

At the close, we realize if we didn't accept it earlier that
Humbert has been living in a dream about Lolita or living out

a dream: Lolita herself never entered the world of his fantasy and she kept her head better, kept a grip on what she was not prepared to accept, kept planning for escape. But if we have questions about damage, we have only to look at the more active choices she has made: her young husband is partially deaf. For this young woman who was once so clear in what she knew and could name, there is no longer any point in having a companion who might hear her, for she has given up that kind of speaking. Instead she calls him 'honey' and does the work of a wife, the work that in circumstances which were economically more favourable her own mother did before her. In fact she is pregnant and on the way to being a mother herself. Lolita's story comes to a close with her death in this first attempt to bear a child; it is as a child that she died to herself much earlier, under our own eyes.

How does Nabokov know about all this, about the web of connection and consequences that he lights up in this story? I find myself wondering why he should be the one who can offer this extraordinarily comprehensive account. Then it comes back to me to remember that Vladimir Nabokov was a naturalist. Ever since the time he was a boy, his passion was for butterflies: to the end of his life, his idea of heaven was a day out in the wild, hunting for them. More than any other writer, it has been said, more even than Goethe, Nabokov was immersed in the world of nature as its student. Though we have been thinking of Nabokov here as an imaginative writer, it is as an expert observer that he was employed at Harvard, as a lepidopterist whose work today carries authority right across the globe. Nabokov learned to observe his surroundings in the natural world in order to pick out the butterflies hidden there and to follow their movements closely enough to capture them. He studied these butterflies in order to bring out and identify the order that connected them and underlay their beauty. It is this power of analytic understanding that he brings to bear in the picture of the human world that he offers in *Lolita*, the story of a girl as ephemeral and open to the world as a butterfly.

When Sandòr Ferenczi encountered an impasse in his own life, refusing to give up what he knew but not understanding how to go forward, he developed an illness, pernicious anaemia, which led to his early death. He observed himself as a doctor and a psychotherapist and recorded what he saw taking place inside.

Nabokov makes a similar connection when he shows Humbert dying of a heart problem. Humbert is unwilling to give up Lolita because he does not know how to live in her absence or in the absence of what she represents for him. For both Ferenczi and Nabokov, as scientific observers, the question stalled on the impasse of masculine identity, the problem of how a man might replace a sense of himself that they knew to be false with one that was more truthful and relied less on the myth of the good father. But Nabokov gets closer to a solution. As a scientist, he puts his finger on the link between fathers and daughters, and on their likeness to each other.

The Bluest Eye
(1970)

Quiet as it's kept, there were no marigolds in the fall of 1941. We thought, at the time, that it was because Pecola was having her father's baby that the marigolds did not grow.

It's the connections that are the mystery in Toni Morrison's story *The Bluest Eye*, the link between one history, one generation and another. There is no secret about what has happened to Pecola. The challenge of how to read Pecola's life, or rather the world in which she was trying to grow up, is what Morrison takes on. That may be why her novel starts with a passage from a child's primer, the book from which children learn to read when they go to school. 'Here is the house. It is green and white. It has a red door. It is very pretty', that primer begins, describing a world that belongs only to people with financial security, an Anglo world of white middle-class people, such as the Mother, Father, Dick and Jane who live in this house. Those names, Dick and Jane, like the shape of the household, exclude the reality of other lives, the lives of immigrants, of the poor and of black people, the households which include lodgers, the families in fragments that we will meet in the course of the story.

Toni Morrison is inviting us to learn about a world to which our eyes may have been closed, perhaps by the very process of education itself. Putting the textbook description under pressure, repeating it, first without punctuation, then without any spaces between the words, speeding it up until the sense collapses,

Morrison asks her readers to give up an old map that only fostered confusion. She will use those run-together strips of nonsense to head parts of her story, as a reminder of the gap between what we have been taught and what we really know if we use our eyes.

Only after this paragraph or so of introduction do we hear the grown-up voice of her narrator, Claudia, who was once Pecola's classmate in school. It is isolated for us, surrounded by white space, filling less than a whole page. There is something that we are to notice about Claudia's account of the world, too: a signal that we might need to distance ourselves from this voice as well. Like the words of the primer, Claudia's words as a grown woman are justified at the right-hand margin, forming a tight fence, a defence, all down the right side of the page. When we come later to a voice whose words are not justified in this way, Claudia's child's voice, we will know to listen differently, perhaps with greater faith in the speaker. This child's voice will pace the story, speaking in chapters named for the seasons, Autumn, Winter, Spring, Summer, rooted in the rhythms of the world. The novel opens with an initiation, or an attempt to undo a much earlier one, the initiation into an accepted way of reading. This new start is a warning, a warning to readers not to believe everything they hear, or at least, like the little girls in the book, to hear the truth in cadences rather than in words, to pause, to look carefully, to interpret for themselves.

Grown-up Claudia speaks of her own guilt and that of her sister, as young girls, of their attempts to pin blame on each other when the marigolds that they planted did not grow. That could sound quite innocent and childlike. But when she claims that there is a connection between Pecola's father, her sister and herself – that like them, he dropped his seeds in his own little plot of black dirt – as readers we have to think again. There is a shock on registering this bitter taste, on taking the full weight of this guilt that seemed so lightly spoken of at first. Leaving the textbook behind we find ourselves flung into the experience which it excludes, flung into the hatred and contempt of self that accompany exclusion. At the same time Morrison forces us to ask what it means to compare these little girls with the father who made his daughter pregnant; she shocks us by insisting even in this context on the link, the commonality between fathers and daughters.

Now we are ready to hear Pecola's story.

It begins in a cold house, the one where Claudia and her sister Frieda were brought up. Pecola joins them there for a few days, brought by a white lady from the county welfare office when her father has made her own family homeless. But while Claudia remembers the poverty and insecurity there that gave the life in that black family a rough edge, she also remembers love, the hands of somebody, her mother, who cared for her when she was sick and did not want her to die. This mother, though, also had another face: she was one of the female relatives, the most powerful one, who carried forward and imprinted on her children the assumption that white was beautiful, that white looks were the ones a black girl should love. Looks that were not her own. At nine years old, Claudia is still fighting off that lesson, furiously dissenting while her older sister and Pecola coo over the picture of Shirley Temple on their favourite cup, just as Claudia sees black women coo in the street after white babies.

Pecola joins the sisters after her father has set fire to the house and put her own family on the street, or put them outdoors, in the language of their own world. It doesn't seem that there is much concern at home to keep Pecola alive. When she arrives she hasn't so much as a change of underwear. Her mother has not spoken to her about menstruation and when she gets her first period at this time a wordless whinny of terror is her response.

On first reading, the time sequence of this novel can seem confusing, moving as it does between many histories and many points of view. From the story that comes through the young girls as they accompany Pecola, the spine of the book, the work will branch out, to trace other lives, her mother's history, her father's story, in order to situate her own. But by starting at the moment of transition between child and woman Morrison chooses to root her book in time, to name a crucial moment, one that she links with the turning point in the psyche, as Claudia names it, the shift when a girl growing up learns to 'love' what she once knew that she hated. Claudia used to hate the blonde baby dolls she was given as ugly, recognizing them as in some way inimical to herself, and to her own body. Her sister and Pecola have moved on to yearning over Shirley Temple. 'Younger than both Frieda and Pecola, I had not yet arrived at the turning-point in the development of my psyche which would allow me to love her. What I felt at that time was unsullied hatred.'

What Morrison is tracing in these girls is the shift to identification with the white myth of the good woman, the perfect mother who keeps the perfect home. Conforming to this myth, or resisting it as the whores do, risks deforming their lives as it has the lives of many of the grown women in the book. The myth has completely taken over the life of Pecola's own mother. In the house of the white people she works for, as we will see, Pecola's mother acts out this white myth; she becomes the good woman who cooks and keeps the perfect house, who tends the white child as the perfect mother. Meanwhile her own daughter, Pecola, is abandoned. Frieda, the sister of Claudia the narrator, who was the same age as Pecola, knew what was going on when Pecola started bleeding, for she had been prepared by her own mother and taught what to expect. Frieda had a sanitary towel ready. She knows too that it means that now Pecola can have a baby. 'Somebody has to love you', she explains. When Pecola asks 'How do you do that? How do you get somebody to love you?', as readers we feel the pain, the huge ignorance, the motherlessness behind her question.

It is now that the parody of the school primer comes into play. Both the chapters that follow are headed with the strip of words from it run together and repeated as they mock the lies about pretty houses and happy families that are taught in school. In this world, for black people the threat of homelessness, of being 'outside', literally excluded, is so real that it makes those who do own a home of their own into frenzied, desperate birds, over-decorating and fussing. 'Propertied people spent all their energies, all their love on their nests.' But Pecola's parents, Pauline and Cholly Breedlove, as we learn, are only renting blacks, very poor ones at that, living in the abandoned store on the south-east corner of Broadway and 35th Street in Lorain, Ohio. Locating their home so precisely, describing its furnishings, tracing the generations of previous occupants, the pizza parlour, the Hungarian baker, the real estate agents, Morrison links their story with the history of immigrant America and its workers. If we thought that in learning about the Breedloves we were going into a secret world, a world none of us knows, where terrible things take place, this description opens our eyes. This family is part of a continuum or rather a web: it is not isolated: its problems, as we begin to understand, are linked with arrangements in a wider social world over which they have no control.

They lived there because they were poor and black and they stayed there because they believed they were ugly, Morrison explains. Replacing the white primer she herself takes the part of the teacher in writing this book. In that sense, she leaves us with only the voice of the ten-year-old Claudia to trust, Claudia who does not claim to understand. Morrison herself speaks as a grown woman who knows, instructing her readers in the effect on the inner lives of black people of the contempt that they meet every day in the eyes of white people. In Pecola's mother, Pauline Breedlove, it becomes a part of her appearance, reinforcing her chosen identity as martyr. In religion Pauline has found a justification for the rage about the life she has been asked to live, rage which she turns on her husband. Trapped as a witness of the fights between her parents, Pecola has already learned to dissociate, to shut off from her body and from feelings that are too painful. Like her mother, Pecola too turns to God for help, asking only to disappear, to lose herself. But whatever she does she can never lose her eyes and what her own eyes have taught her about her mother and about the world. Wanting a different world, she wants different eyes: the blue eyes of the book's title, the winning eyes of a white girl. Pecola is already wanting to unmake herself, body and mind, counting on God to help her as she prays for blue eyes every night.

Later, in the chapter 'Seethemother', we will see how it began, the pattern of dissociation in her mother that left Pecola without support. Pauline satisfies her passion for order by creating the perfect home for the white family which employs her. But as a child it was her art to make arrangements of the household objects that came to hand. She never minded if they were upset, for it gave her a new chance to put them in a different order. Later she missed crayons and colours, as Morrison will tell us, without knowing that she missed them. It was the instincts of an artist that she put into keeping house for her own family when she was a young girl. She enjoyed the quiet house and the garden that she tended when the others had gone off to school. She was not unhappy. Only, longings of a different kind had begun to stir, so that when Cholly Breedlove, gay and handsome, found her standing by the fence one evening, she was ready to leave, to start a new life, make a new home, with a man.

Morrison tells us that Pauline herself, who had been ninth of eleven children, would have said that her life began to go wrong when she was small and a nail went through her foot, leaving her with a limp, or traced it to the moment when as a young wife she broke off a front tooth eating candy in the cinema. She would call herself ugly and blame her unhappiness on that. But Morrison herself offers a different story, one about marriage, of a young woman cooped up in a two-room apartment, lonely in the city, without friends and without a garden to tend, a prisoner and a wife.

At the cinema, Pauline learned to read the world and to know her own place in it. The movies peopled with white stars whom she could not copy gave her release, but only deepened her dissatisfaction with herself and with her husband: '*it made coming home hard, and looking at Cholly hard*', she says (italics in original). When she attempts to channel the tenderness that is leaking away from her marriage, choosing to become pregnant for a second time, she is full of care for the child in her womb as she goes about her work: '*I gone hang up these few rags, don't get froggy*' (italics in original). But once she sees that her newborn baby is a girl, she 'knows' that the child, Pecola, is ugly, rather as Lolita's mother 'recognized' the signs that her own young daughter on the edge of adolescence was bad and stood in need of correction. The city friends who laughed at Pauline's appearance because she could not imitate fashions that were white-led, the movies that blazoned the beauty of white looks, exerted a pressure on her that she had no power to withstand. It meant that when Pauline's daughter Pecola was born, her own mother could not see her beauty.

Upstairs from the Breedloves live the three whores, China, Poland and the Maginot Line, names that resonate with world conflict and with the history of the year 1941 in which the story is set: the names of three lines of defence which did not hold. These women have taken the other path, have resisted becoming good women as a defence against feeling ugly and worthless. Painting their faces, curling their hair, they insist on caring for themselves and making themselves beautiful. But theirs is a resistance which is punctuated by the blues; they have no man of their own and they have no children. Only Claudia's mother, with her angry competence and compunction, stands outside these alternatives, a mother who has not been separated from her children, a wife who shares her life with her husband. Though their mother may whip her daughters she does not ignore their needs like Pauline, nor would she like the Maginot Line 'give them terrible laughs and throw bottles at them', in Claudia's words. The daughters of this far from perfect woman are safe.

But what about men? In the chapter named 'Winter' the voice of young Claudia begins by speaking of her father and the change that comes over him when winter moves with its anxieties 'into his face'. 'Wolf killer turned hawk fighter, he worked night and day to keep one from the door and the other from under the windowsills.' But the boys of her own age that she knows in school show up as enemies, when they turn the racial taunts 'fuelled with their own self-hatred' on Pecola. It takes all Frieda's boldness to defy them and bring that attack to a halt. In this black school all the children are in subtle competition for the favours of Maureen Peal, the middle-class, lightly complected girl with the neat egg sandwiches, the sort of girl who might almost have blue eyes. In the playground shared by Pecola, there are no genuine games, for winning and losing all turn on the question of colour: who is attacked for being black, who is admired for being lighter-skinned. Even the teachers respond differently to Maureen Peal.

Is it the wish to give pleasure that is the mark of the human, of the creature that can be forgiven? Mr Henry, the man who lodges with Claudia's family, makes pets of the girls, calling them after film-stars, giving them pennies. He lies to them too, to get them out of the way when he's entertaining the whores in their mother's house, saying that China and Poland are members of his Bible class. But he gives the girls money to go off and buy ice cream. He tries, later, to fondle Frieda's new breasts and gets chased out of the house by her father, but even after that happens, Claudia tells us 'there was no bitterness in our memories of him'.

What happens to pleasure, asks Morrison, under the conditions of poverty and social exclusion, the conditions that threaten to overwhelm life in this book? It is 'a rainbow between her legs', as Pauline remembers it, even though the days when she could respond to her husband Cholly's love-making are past. Pleasure is right at the heart of the struggling marriage between two damaged people at the centre of the story. It is the link between people, a link that is suggested when the nine pieces of candy that Pecola buys for herself early on are named as nine lovely orgasms. But Pecola is a lonely child and there is no one to share her pleasure. In contrast, Frieda is full of pleasure, energetically taking charge of the situation when Pecola gets her first period

and shouting 'Bury them, dummy', when Claudia wants to know
what to do with the bloodstained panties.

Yet Pecola is going to be destroyed by the end of the story,
destroyed apparently in the context of a man's sexual interest in
her. Wanting to prepare her readers to understand what made
Pecola so vulnerable, wanting to avoid letting them fall into the
trap of seeing her father as sole agent of a magic catastrophe, to
preserve, in fact, some human value in him and even in his act,
Morrison works away, chapter by chapter, at showing how Pecola
is brought down. Leaving the shop of Mr J, who treats her con-
temptuously as a small black girl, she had to 'wait for the inexplicable shame to ebb'. When one boy who singles her out for
attack when she is alone lures her inside his own house to torment
her, his mother delivers another blow. 'Get out', she says, her
voice quiet. 'You nasty little black bitch, get out of my house.'

In explaining this woman, Geraldine, and how she sees in
Pecola the need and the poverty, the helplessness of small black
girls that as a young woman from a home in a quiet well-to-do
neighbourhood, she has escaped, Morrison traces her as representative of a class or rather of a particular style of defence
against the shame of being black. Brown girls, not too dark, who
build their neat homes, their nests stick by stick, making their
own inviolable world closed even against their husbands. Their
children – she says they only have one, a boy – too are kept out
of their hearts, but they may give their love to a pet, perhaps a
cat. It is the hatred that ensues, when her son Junior sees the
love that his mother will give the cat but not himself, that
Morrison uses to start explaining the emotional life of certain
boys. Living in a separation from his mother that is her choice,
Junior is full of cruelty, like his mother the perfect housewife,
'the pretty milk-brown lady in the pretty gold and green house'.
As Pecola turns to find the front door, she sees Jesus looking
down at her 'with sad and unsurprised eyes' from the coloured
picture, in the frame decorated with flowers that gave her such
delight. It's the cruelty of women, including the cruelty of her
own mother with her indifference, allied with the cruelty of a
man of God that will bring Pecola down.

Taking infinite pains to position her readers, Morrison seems to
be preparing us to accept a way of understanding the madness
that overtakes Pecola's mind and leaves her life in ruins as something different from what we might have expected. As she presents

the story, Pecola's madness is not a traumatic consequence of her sexual experience in itself. If that was how Morrison wanted to present it, why bother with all the framing stories about Pecola's mother, about Geraldine with her cat, about Soaphead Church? Why bring us to understand Cholly, the father who raped her?

In this novel, the perfect housewives are separated from their own flesh and blood. Nothing reveals this more clearly than the isolation of sons: Pecola has a brother called Sammy who is famous for running away; she herself has no hope that he would ever take her with him and Sammy is never involved in her story. Geraldine keeps her son Junior at arm's length and in turn he makes himself hateful to other children. As an orphan, Cholly Breedlove lived out an isolation that was more intense. The story of Cholly, the baby who was, like Oedipus, exposed, reveals a breach in the foundations, one which undermines all the lives traced in the novel. At three days old, Cholly was left on a trash heap by his young mother. Growing up, he was cared for by the old woman, Aunt Jimmy, who saved him as an infant. But for Cholly, intimacy was linked with disgust, when he had to sleep in the old woman's bed and carry out her slops. When he succeeds, as a fifteen year old, in finding the man who was said to be his father, he brings all that he has of hope and love to the occasion. The rebuff, when his father shoves him aside to continue with his game of crap, produces a shock that a reader might well register as traumatic, for its impact on him is physiological; standing there in the street he soils himself like a baby. It is this mutilated boy who recovers and goes on to make a life which Morrison will describe ironically as that of 'a free man', one who has no ties. Now we will see how dangerous this European ideal of masculinity really is.

It was not her father who destroyed Pecola, by his action; to read her story this way would be to fall into a trap, a blindness that Morrison wants us at all costs to avoid. All her care goes into showing how the child that her father came on that afternoon was already intensely vulnerable and at risk, a child whose vulnerability could be picked up by anyone looking for a victim. But what Cholly saw, when he came home reeling drunk into the kitchen and found her standing at the sink, was not a victim but a figure, who in its pose and in its extreme youth, reminded him of her own mother at the moment when Pauline's delicacy and fragility had moved him most, the first evening when he found her standing leaning on her gate and had come up behind and nibbled at her ankle. That is the action he repeats now with his daughter: he comes and takes her ankle in his mouth: he tries to go back to an earlier time in his own life, to start again.

As Morrison reminds us at this point, he had no idea of parenting that he could draw on as a model. Instead, as she tells us, he reacted to his children. Having reacted to the visual cue that Pecola offers him, his next move is to respond to the pleasure his contact with her young skin brings. 'I don't know how a man could do it', most readers would probably say. Without Morrison to guide us here, we might, lacking any map to follow or equation to express the dynamic, fall into the error of treating Cholly as a monster, a person whose feelings and actions could not ever be explained in terms that we could recognize. But Morrison has the courage to suggest that we are indeed able to recognize what is happening and to offer her own reading: she does it in terms of memory and of confusion between tenderness and cruelty.

As she describes the scene, it is one where tenderness and cruelty play out alongside each other in his response, which in its immediacy is all that governs Cholly's behaviour. Picking up his daughter's shock, the way Pecola goes rigid under his hands and silent, unlike her mother, Pauline, who had laughed, Cholly, Morrison tells us, finds this response of fear even more satisfying: 'The confused mixture of his memories of Pauline and the doing of a wild and forbidden thing excited him, and a bolt of desire ran down his genitals, giving it length, and softening the lips of his anus.' Cholly is exerting mastery over his own tender feelings as well as over the daughter who brings them back for him – 'He wanted to fuck her – tenderly'– as he rapes Pecola. Tenderness forces him to cover her when he leaves her lying unconscious on the floor.

What did Pecola make of it? Her father can't tell what was meant by the grip of her wet soapy hands on his wrists. Can we tell? After this moment, when Pecola comes to, trying to connect her mother's face as it looms over her with the pain between her legs, there are three more chapters, 'Seethedog,' 'Summer' and 'Looklookherecomesafriend'. With that the book ends, or the picture is complete. If we look back from the turning point of the rape we are reminded that Pecola was already unable to defend herself, already prey to a confusion about her own feelings that she shared with other girls like Frieda. How do the last three pieces of the puzzle, the three closing chapters, complete the picture?

There is a sharp break: the novel starts over, as it were, abandoning Pecola, just as everyone else seems to do, in order to begin a new story: 'Once there was an old man who loved things, for the slightest contact with people produced in him a faint but persistent nausea.' The disgust, the distaste, the unease that were roused in us by the last scene are now harnessed, not to attack Cholly but to be turned on a different target, one which can embody the impersonal forces, such as education, that have proved so destructive – on Soaphead Church, a character who comes on to the stage only at this point.

Pecola enters holding out one of the cards that he uses for advertising: 'Remember, I am a True Spiritualist and Psychic Reader, born with power, and I will help you. Satisfaction in one visit.' When Pecola asks him to give her blue eyes, seeing her as pitifully ugly, he is filled with sympathy. But like Cholly, Soaphead feels his love and sympathy mixed with anger, an anger at his own helplessness, an anger so strong that it feels almost like power. Soaphead does not realize, though we may do, that the pot belly on the little girl is a sign of her pregnancy. Like her father, Soaphead has a story of his own, one shaped by racial history. His story intersects fatally with Pecola's.

An old dog lives down in the yard, sick and disgusting with age: Soaphead has been waiting for revulsion or rage to overcome his distaste in order to get close enough to poison it. Now, he uses Pecola to do the deed, giving her some meat that she does not know is poisoned and saying only that it will be a test: 'If nothing happens, you will know that God has refused you. If the animal behaves strangely, your wish will be granted on the day following this one.' Leaving aside the distress of the old lady who was the dog's owner, it is hard to know whether he is more cruel to the child or to the animal: the dog is killed, but what is done to Pecola? Watching the poisoned dog moving like a broken toy round the yard, she makes a wild pointless gesture with her hand and tries not to vomit. Morrison joins them: Pecola herself will come to jerking and flailing, the movements by which she will come to be recognized as she walks up and down pointlessly for the rest of her life. But before leaving Soaphead, Morrison makes him write a letter to God, justifying himself and what he has done.

This is a bizarre move that the narrative makes: perhaps almost too bizarre for a reader to take in; certainly it will defeat our old habits of reading. Can we believe in Soaphead? Isn't he almost an emblem, quite apart from the feeling that it is too late for a character of any importance to come in? But Toni Morrison would be the last to regret asking for new habits of reading, for she herself is trying to find a new language in order to speak a truth of black American culture. Countering the self-centred old man, with his pious lies, come the young girls who are Pecola's friends. Unlike their elders, from whose overheard gossip they learn that Pecola is having her father's baby, these girls want the baby to live. They know, they sense, the relation between wishing the baby dead and the humiliation that they and their classmates suffer when light-skinned children are preferred. The girls feel the love and pity that everyone else seems to refuse. They bury the money they have been saving for a bicycle and sacrifice the rest of the seeds that they have been selling, planting them themselves, to show God they really mean what they say when they ask him to let the baby live.

Pecola's disintegration is the next thing we know. The final chapter, headed 'Looklookherecomesafriend', takes the form of a dialogue, a dialogue between Pecola and herself. Only as we register, within a dozen lines or so, that they are talking about the eyes that have now turned blue do we understand, sickeningly, that this is not debate but craziness. In the craziness, though, we catch glimpses of reliable information: her mother looks at her drop-eyed, just as we have gathered, from the gossip overheard by the girls, that she beat Pecola savagely when her pregnancy was discovered. Other people avoid looking at her too. Her mother doesn't speak to her, ever. In this utter isolation, the voices in Pecola worry at her experience with her father. Did he make her do it? Was it her fault? Her mother didn't believe her when she told about the rape at the sink. But there was a second time, that she kept to herself, a second occasion at least, when she did not resist:

That was horrible, wasn't it?
Yes.
The second time too?
Yes.
Really? The second time too?
Leave me alone! You better leave me alone. (italics in original)

Soaphead Church, the pious celibate, felt compelled to reach out and touch the bodies of young girls. In the case of Soaphead, the man who is disgusted by other bodies, it is as if his compulsion were re-establishing contact with the human. For Pecola, re-establishing contact with what is human in herself means trying to understand her experience, but, cut off and with no one to talk to, no older woman to explain her body with its response to pleasure to her, Pecola's intelligence turns on itself. Though she has blue eyes now, as she imagines in her delusion, without assurance that she has the bluest eyes, she knows that she is still not safe. The absence of love still presses on her, the absence of respect for what she truly is, even though she cannot interpret it in those terms. In her final reflections, speaking in the voice of Claudia, Morrison suggests that what Cholly gave Pecola was love of a kind: 'He, at any rate, was the one who loved her enough to touch her, envelop her, give something of himself to her.'

The God of Small Things
(1997)

In this, Arundhati Roy's first novel, there is a beloved daughter, but she drowns as a young girl. With *The God of Small Things* the focus shifts onto an absence, opening on a scene of devastation, a family scene, although between us and this devastation stand the novelist and her voice. It is that voice, a voice full of pleasure, which takes us up and transports us to the world of Ayemenem, in South India, to find ourselves among the ruins of a family, just as its daughter Rahel has upped sticks and left America, where she has been living, to come back to Ayenemen as the novel begins. Hearing that her twin brother Estha, whom she last saw when he was sent away at the age of seven, more than twenty years before, has now been sent back, Rahel gives up her job at the gas station and comes home. Before the novel comes to a close, they will make love.

Rahel and her brother are thirty-one years old: the age, she realizes, that 'Ammu', a name that we may not at first recognize as meaning 'mother', was when she died. By the time we do realize this, we have also taken account of another death, the death of Sophie Mol, the young cousin, nearly nine, who died when the twins were seven. It is around that event that a sense of mystery hangs in this first chapter. It is left unexplained yet it is situated, embedded in a scene of family relationships that are broken. At her funeral Sophie's mother, Margaret, refuses to allow the dead child's biological father, her divorced husband Chacko, to put his arm round her in a gesture of comfort. The only gestures of comfort that we hear about during these opening scenes are the nightly creaming of her feet with real cream and the eating of cream cakes that are the habit of Baby Kochamma, the twin's elderly baby grand aunt.

The mystery around the death of Sophie Mol, as it is introduced to us, is thick with hints of violence. Was it a sex crime, we wonder nervously as we read, picking up the references to police stations and to identifying a man? We have learned to connect silence with trauma, the aftermath of unmanageable shock, yet the traumatized person we are shown here, the one who has retreated into silence and walks compulsively about the streets, as Pecola did, is the boy twin – the man twin, rather – Estha. We do get one thing clear about this man who has vacated his own identity, who has embarrassed his parents by taking to doing housework like a servant or a woman: at the bottom of his silence is guilt and the knowledge of treachery. Estha cannot forget that he once told a lie about a man who had treated him only with gentleness. Estha made a false identification of him as an abductor: he remembers a man savagely beaten, beaten to the point of death, who looked at him, and heard when Estha lied 'Yes, this is him.'

'There has been a mistake', Estha's mother said to the officer, when she took her children with her, after the funeral, to the police station where Politeness Obedience Loyalty Intelligence Courtesy Efficiency were spelled out on the wall. If there had been, it was not going to be put right; the children watched as the officer tapped their mother's breasts, 'As though he was choosing mangoes'. 'Police didn't take statements from *veshyas* or their illegitimate children', he said. Roy leaves this word, '*veshyas*', in Malayalam, so that, like young children, we do not understand its meaning but at the same time we know only too well that we do. On the bus, the seven-year-old Estha deals with the conductor and puts his small arms around their stony-faced, weeping mother. Ammu seems to have been traumatized too, for she can't answer the conductor: in this opening chapter we see the pristine closeness between the boy and his mother which has survived in the man of thirty, the son who carries the trauma and the memory for them both.

Only the author with the pleasure of her writing stands between the reader and this apparently alien world. Roy is introducing us to a vision of human behaviour that is disturbing but she is offering it to us as a game, one not so different from the game of the hopeful yellow bullfrogs in search of mates cruising the scummy pond under the monsoon. Her pleasure in the world and in her writing invites us into a sharpened reading, into discarding the false assumptions we might bring and to press forward, wanting to understand what had been really going on in Ayemenem in 1967. And why, as she might put it herself. Just a couple of pages into the novel this riddling, playful voice speaks about the adult twins:

> Edges, Borders, Boundaries, Brinks and Limits have appeared like a team of trolls on their separate horizons. Short creatures with long shadows, patrolling the Blurry End. Gentle half-moons have gathered under their eyes and they are as old as Ammu was when she died. Thirty-one.
> Not old.
> Not young.
> But a viable die-able age.

Like a Kathakali dancer she stamps out her rhythm. This, the death of the mother, is one aspect of the riddle; not a mistake, not a matter of confusion, but a fact. How does the death of the mother fit into the order of things, what is its place in this world based on separation and division?

In Roy's hands the very language will display its own wanton resistance to order and fixity, its movement shifting between conventionally structured sentences and staccato fragments. With its talk of trolls, northern monsters in this Indian text, it will refuse to stay within one system of myth, insist on revealing the input of Europe into what could seem an exclusively Indian problem. As English is spoken in India, which has so many languages of its own, between which speakers move easily, it is fluid and inventive; in India shorts are called 'the half-pant' and meetings that are brought forward can be said to be 'preponed'. Roy turns this freedom, this gay inventiveness with its indifference to orthodox rules, into a bond with her readers, even into her contract with us: when Estha is sent back after twenty-three years by his father, he is said to be 're-Returned'. 'The Loss of Sophie Mol stepped softly round the Ayemenem House like a quiet thing in socks', she tells us: joining in her game with language will let us escape from the confusion in which we begin our reading, the confusion in which we seek like the police, like Baby Kochamma, to put blame on individual men.

For the twins the ground of life had been their mother. They knew her and through her they knew the world. When the words 'A Sunbeam Lent to us Too Briefly' were put on the headstone over the grave of Sophie Mol, it was Ammu who explained, interpreting the world, as she always did for them 'Lent for Too Short a While'. Thanks to her, they knew their own history from the time before they could remember it for themselves. But there was only one photograph which showed the twins as babies with their father; even then, she explained, she had hovered on the fringe of vision, alert to catch them if his unreliable drunkard's arms should let them fall. You could say that the photograph showed the gap where a father should be.

'As ye sow so even shall ye reap', says Baby Kochamma, making it clear that she thinks divine justice lay behind the workings of the past. Comrade Pillai, the old communist, also counts himself free of blame. 'He dismissed the whole business as the Inevitable Consequence of Necessary Politics. The old omelette and eggs thing.' As Roy says, he was essentially a political man. A professional omeletteer. A chameleon who went through the world 'Never revealing himself, never appearing not to. Emerging through chaos unscathed.' Yet between them, the religious woman and the political man, though they considered themselves separate and opposed, had managed to betray each member of the unofficial family that was made up of the Untouchable Velutha and his lover, with her seven-year-old twin children.

In India, Roy suggests, it is hard, as in some other countries, to be allowed to take your own experience as seriously as it deserves. In some countries, like the country Rahel came from, as she puts it, various kinds of despair competed for primacy. Personal despair seems to be trumped by the vast, violent, insane public turmoil of a nation. Having watched as her mother was banished, on her brief return visits Rahel witnessed her gradual disintegration, the sickness that took away her beauty, the coarsened, erratic manner that fails to cover her effort to ward off psychological collapse. After this Rahel grew up without a compass, showing her disturbance at school, so that the teachers whispered it was *as though she did not know how to be a girl*' (italics in original).

She was not likely to want to resemble her disappointed grand aunt or her grandmother who was beaten daily by her own husband; while her mother, who had been a bolder woman, leaving a drunken husband, taking a lover, striking out for a life of her own, had been destroyed. Ammu had refused the model of the good woman: in the novel, she felt she was suffocating in the room where the white mother and daughter were being feted as though they were the only source of light, and from there she stepped out to meet her lover. No wonder if Rahel ran into big girls to find out whether breasts hurt. The emptiness that her husband saw in Rahel's eyes as a grown woman was, according to Roy, a kind of forced optimism, of a type that is brought on in India. How could Rahel take her own despair seriously, howled down as it was by the God of Big Things, the apparently greater claims of a nation poised between the terror of war and the horrors of peace? Yet Roy has chosen to name her novel after the God of Small Things: as readers we are asked to take Rahel's despair as seriously as it merits, even if Rahel herself can't, and to situate what has happened to her in the context of the world in which she has been asked to grow up as a woman.

In common with Morrison, Roy puts a father's feelings for his daughter at the centre of the action, but she does so with a difference. Like Morrison too, Roy stands outside the European tradition in which, none the less, both women were educated. It is out of their resistance to seeing the world through that lens and to seeing themselves, as women, through it that both write. It also involves them in resisting the notion that fathers and daughters are better kept apart. In Roy's story the father, Chacko, loses his nine-year-old daughter Sophie Mol when she is drowned. Going back to the moment of that loss, the novel traces its roots in history and its consequences in the present. In *The God of Small Things* Roy starts from the premise of loss, when the relationship between father and daughter is transformed into a permanent mourning. Roy brings her story to a close in the final chapter with an act that would be named in most societies as incest, though it is not one that could be described as abuse, when a brother and sister, twins, who were separated in the aftermath of Sophie's death, are reunited and make love. It is as if the dynamic set in train by separation is bringing itself to its natural close.

The incest in this story is not abusive but it is linked with trauma, in the sense that it comes about in trauma's aftermath, as an attempt at healing, an attempt to restore close links that have been shattered. The twins Estha and Rahel, the author tells us, make love out of their common sorrow: 'what they shared

that night was not happiness but hideous grief'. In Rahel Estha
sees again his mother's beauty, especially her beautiful mouth,
the mouth that had kissed his hand as he sat in the train that
would take him away from her, the mouth that had promised
that she would come soon, to bring him home. Even as a child,
he registers something wounded-looking about that mouth, as if
it had been struck, or as we might say ourselves, as if it had been
silenced.

> They were strangers who had met in a chance encounter.
> They had known each other before Life began.

Roy offers two different ways of reading what the twins were to
each other. But when Rahel kisses her brother's hand, she is re-
enacting the scene at the train-side where they were separated,
when she was left screaming doubled-up on the platform. Their
act of love in the present might be an attempt to get back before
that time.

It is to the attempt to regulate love, to the making of the Love
Laws, as Roy calls them, that she traces the far-off beginning of
her story: 'it really began in the days when the Love Laws were
made. The laws that lay down who should be loved, and how.
And how much', she explains as her novel opens. Any reader
might easily misconstrue this, taking it for a hint that a sexual
relationship between family members would be at stake. It is
true that the twins, reunited as grieving, traumatized adults do
have sex: 'Emptiness was entered by Quietness', as the novel
tells it. But rather than putting a technical contravention, this
sorrowful coupling between coevals and equals, at the centre, it
is violence, a violence that is hidden under the name of law, and
endorsed or condoned in the name of religion that Roy wants to
address. This violence is linked with the system of caste, the
hierarchy that is enshrined at the heart of Indian life and for ten
thousand years has regulated whom people may marry. This involves silencing the voice of desire in men as well as in women:
'An old man's mouth in a young man's face', the face where the
teeth have been broken by police brutality, is the image that
haunts the imagination of Estha, the man twin.

At some time in his growing up, almost imperceptibly, Estha
had withdrawn into silence. At thirty-one, he has been living for
years in an inner world where there is no language. Yet he cannot

get rid of the images brought by memory. Estha remembers the broken body of Velutha, the skilled craftsman whom the twins had loved to the point of worship, the man who, though they did not know it, had become the lover of their mother, Ammu, in the days before he died. As one who came from the caste of Untouchables, Velutha stood in the place of greatest vulnerability in his society, even though he lived in Kerala, said to be the most advanced of Indian states, with its Marxism and its high degree of literacy. When Sophie Mol could not be found, what was easier for a bitter and envious old woman, the aunt, Baby Kochamma, who had learned of the love between Ammu and himself than to throw the blame on Velutha? As a child of seven, Estha was taken to identify the barely conscious Velutha in the cells.

Still as a man of thirty Estha remembers how Velutha opened one bloodshot eye, 'smiling, with some unhurt part of him at the sight of this beloved child', and looked at Estha as Estha said 'Yes.' This 'Yes', the syllable that betrayed Velutha, is the word that the octopus inside Estha, which has gradually eaten up all his language, cannot extract. Even at seven he had known that it was an act of betrayal and that he was telling a lie in claiming that Velutha had abducted the children the night Sophie Mol had drowned. But it was the only way to save his mother from jail, Baby Kochamma had falsely sworn. How could Estha have known that Baby was afraid that she herself was going to be charged for filing a misleading report? The police officer, caught with the death in custody of a man against whom no charge had been made, leaned on Baby Kochamma and she leaned in her own way on the twins. Caught between two loves that she had made to seem contradictory, loving the man who played with them and loving their mother, the desperate children had chosen their mother. It was Estha, the less able to resist her, whom his aunt chose to make the formal identification.

Trauma stands at the centre of the world that Roy is creating, but it is not a trauma that is mainly caused by sexual abuse, though that might be said to play a part. It is said that one instance of abuse makes a child more liable to be victimized; the child that was chosen to do Baby Kochamma's dirty work was a boy who had been sexually molested, when the Orangedrink Lemondrink Man at the cinema had forced him to suck his penis. But in the world that Roy sees, this abuse only lays the ground for an act of moral abuse. When Baby pressures Estha into lying and so betraying both himself and the man who loved him, she lights the slow fuse of the process by which Estha gradually silences himself. Giving up speaking looks like the response of shame, a way of punishing himself for that 'Yes' that could never be unsaid.

This story starts by making the reader know the worst and that it has already happened. Just as flashbacks ask individuals to pay attention to the wound in their past and to take up and own the unclaimed experience that trauma represents, this novel asks us as readers to know. The sense of mystery which hangs around the death of Sophie Mol as the novel opens will turn out to have been mere confusion, a mistake that has been contrived, like the false identification Estha made. This mistake is a deliberate one that we are invited into making, only in order that we may realign our notions with greater clarity. From the start Roy invites us to recognize links that might otherwise go unsuspected, links between the world of institutionalized religion and the misery that has been created in this family. In the first chapter Baby Kochamma's story as the daughter of a Syrian Christian priest is laid out. The experiences which have deformed her, leaving her with such a will to destruction, are carefully traced: central to these is her profound sense of betrayal.

As a woman she has been denied appropriate recognition and response: the name Roy has chosen for her, Baby, reflects this. When we first see her Baby Kochamma is an old lady with dyed black hair, squeezing the thick, frothy bitterness out of an elderly cucumber. As a young girl she had fallen in love with an Irish monk, Father Mulligan, who could recognize, as her own father did not, the tide of sexual excitement that rose in her in his presence. Baby gave up her own religion to become a Roman Catholic and went into a convent, but she found that it did not bring her any closer to Father Mulligan. Years later she discovered that he had succumbed to temptation and left the priesthood for another woman. Baby became obese and the garden that she spent fifty years in tending round her father's house was a bitter one.

It could be a fairy-tale, this story, so clear are its images of a desire to punish that has been nurtured over many years. Baby does not know that this is driving her when she sets the police on Velutha. But for Roy there is a manifest connection between the violence which is unleashed by Baby Kochamma and the denial, the refusal to acknowledge her as a woman, which she has encountered at the hands of Christian priests. After it was all over, Baby Kochamma said 'As ye sow, so also shall ye reap', as if she had had nothing to do with the sowing and the reaping. Picking up the voice of the priest, she also adopts their refusal to know.

In India, caste divides the community, supposedly along the lines of a set of ancient professions, with the priesthood occupying the highest rank. In doing so, like Christianity, it hampers clear thought, perhaps, Roy suggests, in ways beyond those we are familiar with. When it trains the mind to view people primarily in terms of groups which are separated from each other, caste-thinking overrides the evidence of close connection. This move is one which Roy as novelist refuses to accept. She does not stop at telling a love story that crosses the line of caste: more radically, she tells a story that reveals caste as an institution, which like the institution of taboo fosters mental confusion. In her epigraph, she quotes John Berger: 'Never again will a single story be told as though it's the only one'; she chooses to write about a brother and sister who are twins. Even as an adult, after twenty years of forced separation, Estha knew without being told when his sister had come back. As a child, Rahel, Estha's twin sister, had shared his life so closely that she woke laughing at his dreams: she knew what the Orangedrink Lemondrink Man had done to her brother in Abilhash Talkies, just as she knew the taste of the tomato sandwiches that he had eaten on the Madras mail, on his long journey away from her at seven. Into this shared knowledge, this intimacy, cut the defining separation between them which came after Sophie Mol's death: the Edges Borders Boundaries Brinks and Limits which also separated them from their mother. It is as though the dividing lines that are symbolized in India by caste and are meant to prevent any crossing of thought or feeling were materializing within families too.

Which brings us to Chacko. Chacko was already ruined, in a limited sense, before the death of Sophie Mol, his daughter. It started with his upbringing as a spoiled, helpless Indian son. In a country where every possible difference was made between daughters and sons, Chacko was waited on by women yet choked by their dependence on him. In this instinctive revulsion a basic health in him that refused to die away asserted itself.

It is Chacko's instinct for life that makes him so loveable, in spite of the shortcomings that make him maddening. Recognizing his responsiveness, a responsiveness that is most graphically demonstrated in his surrender to his little daughter, we are the more appalled by the blind cruelty he turns to in his despair. He is the one responsible for sending Ammu and her children away. Roy has so contrived her story that it combines exposé and affirmation: it exposes the disasters created in the name of an order that is patriarchal while it makes affirmation of the love which is to be found in men. One of these loving men, who know how to take the part of a father, teaching the children around them how to live, is Velutha, the Untouchable: the other is Chacko. The swimming lessons which he gave to Rahel and Estha saved their lives, while his own daughter, Sophie Mol, who was brought up without him, drowned.

Paradoxically, it is Velutha who has a wider range of useful experience to pass on. In Chacko, Roy presents one who has been made helpless by the upbringing and by the elite education that were designed to advantage him as a man. He had been a Rhodes Scholar, singled out for his intelligence, just as he had been singled out by his birth into a family of means. But the education that he received at Oxford, as one of the Rhodes Scholars, the group of privileged male undergraduates selected from the former colonies under the terms of a foundation set up in memory of Cecil Rhodes and given three years at Oxford as a final polish, was one that finally disabled him for living in the world.

Chacko could not divest himself of his early training in order to meet English notions of what a man was: he simply had never learned to do things for himself. When his marriage to the English girl, Margaret, who had thrilled him by refusing to cling to him, failed and he went back to India, Chacko found that his liberal education was not much use to him. When he took over his mother's business, Paradise Pickles, it promptly began to go downhill. His education had taken him away from the world of action, leaving him only with a supply of reflective observations that came between Chacko and his experience of the world.

'Anything's possible in Human Nature', Chacko said in his Reading Aloud voice. Talking to the darkness now, suddenly insensitive to his little fountain-haired niece. Love. Madness. Hope. Infinite joy.

Chacko understood something about women and oppression. He had stepped in when he discovered that his father was beating his mother. But though his sympathies were given to the workers, in the event this political impulse drained away in the flirtatious chats he would have with the women from the factory in his office, urging them to pursue their rights. In a sense it was a final betrayal on the part of his mother when she had a door cut in the side of the house so that the women who came to sleep with him should be more easily overlooked by the rest of the household: she did it in recognition of what she termed a Man's Needs.

What this man needed, most of all it seems, was his daughter. No one taught him that, but he knew. When Rahel asked him, as a child, if he loved Sophie Mol more than anything else in the world, 'She's my daughter', he said. That was all. Though her mother had asked him for a divorce soon after Sophie was born, and Chacko had had to move out, before he left her, he would get up in the night to memorize his sleeping child, 'To learn her.' Even though he could not resist scanning her for resemblance to the other man whom his wife now loved, his wonder at her overcame his jealous desire for ownership.

> She smelled of milk and urine. Chacko marvelled at how someone so small and undefined, so vague in her resemblances, could so completely command the attention, the love, the *sanity* of a grown man.
>   When he left, he felt that something had been torn out of him. Something big.

His heart remained generous: when Joe, the other man for whom his wife had left him, was killed in an accident, he invited his ex-wife to bring his daughter and stay for Christmas. Watching the preparations of this man to receive them, his careful dressing, the purchase of two red roses, and observing the mismatch between his offers of love and their response is almost too painful. 'Uh do you mind putting me down?', asks Sophie Mol when Chacko hugs her as if he would never let her go. Without her to love, his despair can break out as it does in the act of violence which shatters the door of his sister's room. 'Pack your things and go', he says, stepping over the debris to their mother Ammu in the presence of the terrified twins.

The Rhodes Scholarships, the prize that crippled Chacko, were set up for the purpose of 'promoting unity among the

English-speaking nations': at the time when he was given one and until 1976 they were only offered to unmarried males between the ages of nineteen and twenty-five from countries that Britain had colonized, which suggests that it was also to promote the ideal of white masculinity on a world-wide basis that they were set up. Perhaps it is not an accident that both Toni Morrison, writing as an African-American, and Arundhati Roy, when they ask about relationships that are forbidden, set their stories in a public history of catastrophe, one that has already happened. This public history of slavery and of colonization provides the explanatory background that is lacking in Bergman's *Through a Glass Darkly* or only implied in Williams's *Suddenly Last Summer*. And though *Lolita* appears to focus on personal history, it was noticeable that in the remake a black woman was introduced in the form of a helper employed by Lolita's mother. This black woman was the only person to express scepticism about Humbert.

In the distant imaginings of Europe, the Greeks had a story that human lives were controlled by the Fates as they sat at their spinning, ancient women who could cut off the thread of a man's life at will. That speaks for the vulnerability felt by men and of their fear of what could be done to them by mothers, the mothers who have been taught to turn away. The link is clearer now between that old story and Europe's newer fiction, the one taught at Oxford and perhaps at other universities and colleges, the story that the spindle of white masculinity was what made the world turn. Now it is possible to understand the abuse and the violence that keep cropping up in one shape after another as deformations that are bound up with the attempt to keep that story going and to promote the idea of men as separate creatures. The view of closeness between fathers and daughters as horribly suspect, a view that is reinforced in the light of anxieties about sexual abuse, now seems to me like a part of the same confusion. Looking at his baby daughter, Chacko recognized that she commanded his sanity as a man. This turned out to be no exaggeration, for when he lost her the feelings that she had kept alive in him, feelings tuned to wonder in the face of vulnerability and to delight, gave place to a violence that swept away the lives of his sister and her children.

Conclusion

One way of linking the different forms which are taken by abuse is to say that they make up a continuum of cruelty. This connection is important: yet it seems even more urgent to point out that they are related structurally. The damage caused to children under the taboo on tenderness, which prepares them to live in a world which separates out fathers, is the place where the forms of adult sexuality are laid down. The reliance on cruelty as a route to pleasure, as in sadism, or on subservience, as masochism requires, looks back to that formative experience. When the sexual abuse of children or minors takes place this behaviour also looks back to that same threshold, the moment of forced removal into an alien world.

The church is not the only institution which has given a place to cruelty. Other institutions enshrine it too, particularly cruelty against children, very often in the name of law and order or of social responsibility. I am thinking of the mothers who are imprisoned for relatively minor offences, separating them from their young children, and of the adolescents who kill themselves while in detention or awaiting trial. I ask about the blind impulse behind the social planning which allows so many children to grow up in poverty.

When a new scandal over child abuse in regulated foster homes is brought to light or a fresh example of failure to act in the face of signs of abuse on the part of those charged with responsibility occurs, every time and without fail the authorities pronounce that there must be no more of these lapses of responsibility and that 'lessons must be learned'. Hearing this echo of the classroom with its lesson of blindness and silence, I do wonder. It makes it harder to be optimistic: the language reminds me too much of the old story with its reliance on punishment and blame. But at the same time, encouragingly, the public response to these scandals reveals that there is at least as much widespread anger against the system that fails to protect children as there is against those individuals who harm them. The impulse to question those in authority is the first step towards questioning the social order in itself; a step too towards recognizing that abuse is not an aberration from regular social order but quite the reverse: abuse is an end product of the social order that we have come to accept.

Under ordinary circumstances, such a radical perspective does not come easily to the individual. Education does not usually encourage us to use our own experience to challenge the ways in which it has taught us to think; that kind of evidence is loftily dismissed as 'anecdotal'. We don't always know how to make the link between our personal experience and the theoretical work of analysts, or between theory and the picture of the world that is shown to us by art. In spite of all that I myself knew in theory, it was only recently that I learned from my brothers that like Laurent they had been intimately approached by the priests in their boarding school. In writing this book, however, I have attempted to close those gaps, making use of what I have observed for myself in conjunction with theory, comparing the two. At the same time I have been comparing both with the vision of the world that is offered by artists, picking up the resonances there.

'When I became a man, I put away childish things', St Paul wrote. 'Children should be seen and not heard', as they used to say. But what we once knew as children is not so easily to be escaped: today western societies seem to be obsessed by the image of the child. Photographs of children catch our eyes everywhere from galleries to magazines: many viewers have been troubled by the poise in these images between vulnerability and sexual appeal, feeling that they are an invitation to abuse, or even an endorsement. Let me suggest that there might be another way of seeing these photographs, one that was not governed by the old reflexes of guilt and blame. Closing up the gap between sexuality and the tenderness that is children's due, these images might well be viewed as mute reminders, taking each of us back to a connection that has been all but forgotten, the connection between our loss of the tenderness we knew as children and our fears as adults.

Seeing the prevalence of these images, noting the perturbation they provoke, I wonder. I ask myself whether, as a society, we are almost ready to lend an ear to those inner voices that speak to us of what we learned in childhood, what we learned long ago and still cannot help but know. Or are we going to choose to ignore those agitating reminders and draw back once again from what we most deeply know?

Notes

The internet has made bibliographical searches so easy that I have chosen to offer only abbreviated publication details here.

Introduction

Intimacy and Pleasure

Page 2   **the writer Anton Chekhov**: in a letter to A. S. Suvorin, 27 October 1888.

Page 10   **a recent survey**: *Voices from the Silent Zone* published in New Delhi, September 1998, was conducted by the group entitled Recovery and Healing from Incest (RAHI), director Anuja Gupta.

Page 14   **the study of refugee children that he made**: *Maternal Care and Mental Health: A Report Prepared on Behalf of the World Health Organisation as a Contribution to the United Nations programme for the Welfare of Homeless Children*, 1952.

Page 17   **his 1935 book**: republished in 1988 by Free Association Books with a foreword by John Bowlby and reprinted in 1999. See in particular chapter VI, 'The Taboo on Tenderness'.

Mystification

Page 22   **Robin Fox, the anthropologist**: in his book *The Red Lamp of Incest*.

Page 23   **Freud situated the taboo on incest at the centre of individual emotional life**: 'Some Psychical Consequences of the

Anatomical Distinction between the Sexes' (1925), *Standard Edition* vol.19.

Page 27   **From the beginning of the nineteenth century breeders of stock animals were discounting the so-called dangers of inbreeding**: as discussed by Harriet Ritvo in her book *The Platypus and the Mermaid*.

Page 29   **When priestly castes in ninth-century Persia encouraged men to take their daughters and nieces, even on occasion their own mothers, as their wives**: reported by Walter Scheidel in 'Brother–Sister and Parent–Child Marriage Outside Royal Families in Ancient Egypt and Iran: A Challenge to the Sociobiological View of Incest Avoidance?', *Ethology and Sociobiology* (1996), 17.5.

Jennifer Montgomery: *Art for Teachers of Children*

Page 56   **she told an interviewer**: see the interview with Montgomery, 'Memories of Sexual Violence', *Film Quarterly* (1996–7), 50.2, winter.

Sappho Durrell

Page 62   **In 1991 the magazine *Granta* carried an edited selection**: 'Journals and Letters', *Granta* (1991), n.s. 37. It is not always clear which parts of this edited text are taken from journals and which from letters.

Father Porter and Cardinal Law

Page 70   **the case against Father James Porter**: the details of this section are all drawn from reports published in the latter part of 1992 in the *Boston Globe*. In July 2001 the *Globe* was carrying reports that Cardinal Law was being cited for negligence in connection with the case of another abusing priest. By March 2002 this scandal had assumed international proportions.

Sandòr Ferenczi and Sigmund Freud

Page 79   **That paper is now recognized as the classic discussion of incest**: 'The Confusion of Tongues between Adults and the Child' (1933), reprinted in Ferenczi's book *Final Contributions to the Problems and Methods of Psycho-analysis*, 1955.

Page 80   **the clinical diary that he had been keeping since the beginning of the year**: *The Clinical Diary of Sandòr Ferenczi*, edited

by Judith Dupont and translated by Michael Balint and Nicola
Zarday Jackson, was published in 1988.

Valerie Sinason and Estela Welldon

Page 91   **she tells us**: the published work of Welldon's that I draw on
for this section includes the 20th S. H. Foulkes Lecture,
Estela V. Welldon, 'Let the Treatment Fit the Crime: Forensic
Group Psychotherapy', published in *Group Analysis* (1997),
30, and 'Group Therapy for Victims and Perpetrators of
Incest', *Advances in Psychiatric Treatment* (1998), 4.

Page 91   **in her essay, 'Interpretations that Feel Horrible to Make'**:
Journal of Child Psychotherapy (1991), 17.

Suddenly Last Summer (1959)

Page 119   **her essay on women who abuse**: 'Women as Abusers' in
K. Abel, M. Buszewicz and S. Davidson (eds), *Planning Community Mental Health Services for Women*, 1996. See also her
book *Mother, Madonna, Whore: The Idealisation and Denigra-
tion of Motherhood*, 1988.

Index

voice, voices (*cont.*)
  in *The God of Small Things* 164
  loss of as sign of trauma 39,
    41, 67–9
  mother's 51, 60
  of priests 29, 172
  of textbook 58
  and theatre 13
Voices from the Silent Zone 179n

war 47
  First World War 18
  Second World War 9, 10, 14, 77

Welldon, Estela 78, 90, 91,
  94–7, 119, 181
Wheeler, Charles 10
white, whiteness
  see also race 123, 175
Williams, Rose 108
Williams, Tennessee 101,
  107–23, 175
Winters, Shelley 139
Woman in a Dressing-Gown
  40
women 14, 24, 29, 32, 68, 76,
  156–7, 167–8